THE JESUITS IN MODERN TIMES

The Jesuits in Modern Times

By

JOHN LaFARGE, S.J.

THE AMERICA PRESS
New York
1928

Imprimi potest:

LAURENCE J. KELLY, S.J.,
Provincial Maryland-New York.

Nihil obstat:

ARTHUR J. SCANLAN, S.T.D.,
Censor Librorum.

Imprimatur:

PATRICK CARDINAL HAYES,
Archbishop of New York.

December 17, 1927.

TABLE OF CONTENTS

INTRODUCTION

THE reflections which are embodied in the following pages represent certain impressions received of the Jesuit ideal, not as a matter of abstract theory, but in actual practice, by one who became a member of the Order after abundant experience of the world and of non-Catholic education, and after long opportunity to study the workings of the Jesuit life close at hand, with the impartial eye of an outside observer. Though the earlier impressions have developed and amplified, yet the give and take of life in the Order have never altered their essential qualities.

Long hours of lonely traveling in a country mission gave opportunities for meditation on certain proportions and connections that might have been passed over in a more crowded life. The book, however, does not treat *ex professo* or officially with the Institute of the Order, or with the Canon Law of the Church as applied to the Order. It simply means to show what one secular priest found in the Society of Jesus in addition to his own priestly ideals.

Even for the general reader there is some interest in such a characterization of Jesuit life. Contact with the Catholic Church means sooner or later some form of contact with the Jesuits, either through writings, through preaching, or by meeting with individuals. Such contact will arouse the question: what is the significance of the Jesuit in the present age? Is he simply a survival, an anachronism, or does he stand for something helpful and constructive? He is a man with a rational goal of life in an age when most people are drifting. Does his goal, or the means he takes to attain it, have any value for the average man?

Most of the misunderstandings and misrepresentations of the Jesuit life and aims, in the author's opinion, come from misunderstandings as to the true nature of the Religious life as such. Rarely, indeed, if ever, does he meet with criticism from men who have attained a deeper understanding of the spirit common to all the Orders of the Catholic Church. In fact his most understanding friends may be members of communities which in appearance and field of activity are widely different from that of the Jesuit. Hence a good part of these papers is taken up with simply the Religious life as such, approached, however, from a Jesuit angle.

The terms "Jesuit" and "Religious" are a good deal interchanged. Without adhering to any strict rule in the matter, the term Religious has generally been used when the remarks seemed to apply to other Religious communities than the author's own. On the other hand, at least to avoid monotony, the term Jesuit is used to describe specifically Jesuit ideas. With the interchange and intermingling of spiritual ideals and ascetic practices that have occurred especially in the growth of more recent Religious communities, hard and fast distinctions are apt to be misleading or invidious. Anyone venturing on such topics must ask to be understood simply as trying to record what he has found good, without any idea of appropriating for the few what is common to many or to all.

The little book is neither an historical treatise nor an apologia. It is not controversial. For points of controversy, if the reader is interested in them, reference may be made to the standard works treating of the Society. Little new will be conveyed to the well-instructed Catholic, nor is the book intended to appeal even to the average reader. It is addressed rather to those persons who, though versed in current issues and alive to current ethical and social discussions, have yet to find an informal presentation of the Jesuit's aim in life in the terms characteristic of such discussions in our time and country.

Personal reminiscences would have greatly helped to illustrate and confirm the statements herein made. Numberless such instances, both from personal acquaintances and from history, occurred to the writer. Since, however, his purpose was merely to make a concise characterization, and not to furnish a record of achievements, he has thought better to omit all but a few particularly needed for special illustration of his meaning.

In the first chapter, treating of "Vocation," the Jesuit way of life is seen to present itself to man as one of the possible means of realizing to its greatest extent the fulness of life, as attainable through the teaching, the example and the grace of Christ. Compliance with this vocation is shown as a decision to share Christ's apostolic enterprise on earth, by joining with others similarly inclined, according to a traditional observance, in order to share in a special manner the conditions of Christ's earthly life, as expressed in the Counsels of Poverty, Chastity and Obedience.

In the second chapter, these Counsels are shown as the pathway to spiritual freedom, the difference being pointed out between the unobligated practice of their characteristic virtues and the definite commitment to such a practice as a perpetual rule of life. Obedience, with its motives, and constitutional limitations both of scope and exercise is treated of in the third chapter.

The characteristics of the Jesuit apostolate are shown in chapters four and five, the latter discussing Catholic higher education as the most prominent Jesuit activity in the United States. In the following chapter six, the inner life of the Jesuit is described, first in its relation to external activity, which is illustrated especially in the instances of the Jesuit Lay Brother; then, its relation to the priestly ideal as such. The concluding chapter defines the Jesuit position towards the world, and conjectures as to the well-known opposition which the Jesuit Order has always experienced.

In order to attain precision and brevity of statement, a few technical terms are used throughout, although in general the language tries to be as untechnical as possible.

The word Religious, spelt with a capital, refers to the member of an Order or of a Congregation, as established by a definite mode of life, Vows, and canonical sanctions. Otherwise, spelt with a small *r*, it retains its usual meaning. Hence we speak of a Religious man (a member of such an Order), in quite a different sense from that of a "religious man": a man who practices religion. Order is used of a community if its vows are recognized by the Church as solemn; if known only as simple vows, it is called a Congregation.

The same proviso attaches to certain other words spelt with capitals, all of which apply specifically to the life of a Religious community, as contrasted with their ordinary meaning. Such are:

Order. (He belonged to the Carmelite Order; but he gave an order for ham.)

Vows. (The monk keeps his Vows; but the sailor's vow was kept.)

Observance. (The Dominican Observance; but the observance of the traffic laws.)

Rule. (The Rule of St. Benedict; but the rule of using commas.)

Constitution. (The Constitutions written by St. Ignatius; but don't ruin your constitution.)

Superior. (The Superior of the monastery; but a superior method of cultivation.)

Brother. (A Franciscan Brother; but my brother and sister are in town.)

Counsels. (The Counsels of the Gospel; but my counsel was to avoid the cold.)

Poverty, *Chastity*, and *Obedience*. (As a matter of the observance of a Religious community, as such.)

The Jesuits in Modern Times

CHAPTER I

VOCATION

I

A LITTLE book happens to hand at the beginning of this chapter. "Three Thousand Occupations" are described, which are open to every young American. Everything you ever heard of is listed therein, and ten times more that you have never heard mentioned. You have the choice of sausage mixer and piccolo player, museum curator and lion farmer, rhinologist and Army Inspector General. Various kinds of "religious work" are described: minister, curate, pastor, bishop, cardinal, even the Pope. But no suggestion is made of becoming a Jesuit, or any other type of Religious, priest or lay, except a "nun."

If the thought of a Religious Order for men did occur to the compiler of this manual, it would probably be dismissed as impractical, since, as in the case of the nun, there is "no remuneration, except convent bed and board." It is not a business opportunity; and American young men are supposed to be looking for something that will pay. Nevertheless, realistic and practical as are our age and country, a false note is struck when we declare that American youth has no sense but for the material. If the non-material standard seems impractical to many of the older generation, there are as many of the younger men to whom a merely material standard seems unreal, as not based on life as it appears to them.

The older man if not a philosopher and a mere theorist, may catalogue all things human under the rigid columns of profit and loss. For him, achievement is a past dream, laid aside with silver tennis trophies and class photographs.

The average young American, however, who has some broader outlook due to education, and who is not of the drifting or sheep-like variety, may not be much interested in philosophies and abstract ideals. Conscious adherence to a "movement" is apt to give him the creeps. But he does want to achieve something. The United States is still the land of achievement, and it will remain such for many years to come. Some explaining may be needed to convince him that certain supposed achievements are not achievement at all, but mere blowing of soap bubbles; but the desire does not have to be implanted. It is in the character of youth, and in the air of our own country.

Moreover, as a man among men, and as a young man in particular, he is, as a rule, not attracted by the idea of solitary achievement, without relation to others. The vision of the Lone Eagle may drift across his imagination for the moment, but common sense will make him look for a leader and companion in adventure and achievement.

If we could sum up the elements of life that seem most precious to a young man who can look beyond bread, butter and pleasure, we may say that they are: the opportunity of achievement; a real leader to follow; and companions in high adventure. Love, sport and battle, art, science, exploration, business, politics and the whole world of human affairs each offers its own possibilities of adventure and achievement. In each the leader can be found, in each the group of companions inspired by the same enthusiasm. But each, too, has its limits, both in time and the current of human energy, as well as in the scope they can attain, even at the height of a very problematic success.

On the other hand the more that the whole of life is looked upon as an opportunity, the more that the whole scheme and texture of life is to be swung into one complete achievement, the more a young man feels the moral division, the disintegration that is at work in life as he actually begins to find it. The formulas do not fit; the castles do not build; the opportunities vanish as he approaches them. Routine for adventure, passivity for action, calculation for sincerity, concealment for frankness, policy for ideals, compromise for achievement, unwilling drifting with the herd for high companionship in exploit, subservience for loyalty: such is the antinomy, the cleavage that pierces a man's heart. If it is not healed nor healable, it dissolves a man into skepticism, and paralyzes endeavor, or drives him into moral isolation.

There is no need of illustration of either the state of things or the sentiment that they provoke; young men's literature of today is keyed enough, as it is, on that one stop of the *Vox Dolorosa*.

Is there an opportunity, therefore, for an achievement which will not only resist this disintegrating influence, this death-in-life, but which will entirely triumph over it, which will utilize the very obstacles, the very elements that naturally drive stream-downward, to push stream-upward to the very fountain-head of life's accomplishment? There are plenty of answers to this question, but I have no idea of retailing them, much less discussing them here. Every religion, every philosophy has something on the matter. Since this little book is only a characterization, not a defence or apologia, I merely note that this is the claim of the Jesuit ideal; or, to be more precise, the Religious ideal as conceived according to the Jesuit tradition. It is thought of as an opportunity for achieving the fulness of life, by personally following, in a special and distinctive manner, the guidance of the Son of God, as the great Captain of human endeavor, in the high companionship of brothers bound to a like enterprise on earth and of triumphant brethren in Heaven.

II

How far is such a notion attainable by the modern mind, which demands that the ground be tried before it steps, and is too disillusioned by the past to take chances with the future? Let us be frank, for otherwise we are using simply meaningless terms, and the whole affair may be judged merely as unintelligible. It is not necessary to be a Catholic to conceive the Jesuit ideal in its general and larger aspects. But it is necessary to be a Catholic to accept it, since it has profoundly Catholic implications. Moreover, it is necessary for that very reason, to reckon with those implications in trying to understand it.

We can sum up these Catholic implications under two or three headings.

In the first place we presuppose, what is not peculiar to Catholics, that we look upon Christ as a Divine guide to human endeavor. In other words, we admit the possibility that Christ can offer a practical suggestion as to unifying and integrating my life, and we assume that His suggestion will be of supreme value, owing to His unique nature and office. For it is not a question here of precepts and commandments, but of suggestions and ideals.

Moreover, we suppose, what is also not unique for Catholics, that His teachings are conveyed to us, over the period that has elapsed since His earthly life, by the action of the Divine Spirit, continuing and confirming the teaching office of Christ in the teaching office of His Church, which Church He authorized to deliver His teaching to all ages and to all individuals.

If, however, anything is obvious from the Gospel, it is that Christ definitely undertook to restore men to inner unity and fulness of life by uniting them with God His Father, the Author of that life. The same idea is presented in varying terms.

To the Samaritan woman at the Well of Jacob He offered "living water," reminding us of the thirst that the higher nature of every man feels for some such restoration and fulness of life, and of the working of the Holy Spirit as the fountain of supernatural grace.

He announced that He came that men might have life, and have it more abundantly. In His high-priestly prayer, at the Last Supper, He asked His Father to "make holy" (sanctify) His disciples. Yet holiness was to be obtained not through formalism or outward observances, but by spiritual union with God, the all-holy.

To the Rich Young Man, who expressed his sense of inner incompleteness, "What is yet wanting to me?" He replied by using the term "perfect," as the complement of incompleteness, and showed him what he must do, if he wished to remove *all* incompleteness, all inner contradiction, from his life.

Whether we say holiness, or perfection, or restoration, or self-integration, there is here an underlying concept, in the moral order, which is one of the suppositions of Christianity. Without it, neither the Jesuit Order nor the Religious or priestly ideal could exist.

The non-Catholic reader, if there be such, may not agree with this view. Nor am I here undertaking any demonstration of its correctness. I am simply asking him to register it mentally, as essential for his understanding of the Jesuit ideal: for without such understanding all subsequent explanations are meaningless. The same proviso applies to what follows.

For this ideal is presented to the modern man not as coming from a person wholly identified with a past epoch, but as proposed by one physically, personally present. Christ, as Saviour, Redeemer and Counselor, is looked upon, by the eye of Catholic Faith, as present in the Sacrament of the Holy Eucharist, not only present, but making His presence felt by the action of His Holy Spirit. By means of this action of the Holy Spirit, the grace, or special help, is given to the individual first, to have a clearer, more spiritual understanding of life and its problems than would he otherwise attain; and secondly, to receive that inward strengthening of his will, that fortification of his own character, which is necessary in order to put Christ's proposition into practice.

From both these suppositions we see that the idea of the Religious vocation flows from the basic concepts of Catholic teaching. Its realization in the individual results from the practice of the sacramental, the corporate life of the Church. Through his sharing in the mysterious spiritual life, which flows to every member of the Church as the mystical body of Jesus Christ, he is brought into direct, personal and effective relationship with Christ, as the Head of that Body, and is fitted to sit at His feet and to choose the "better part."

III

What then is the nature of this invitation, on the offering and acceptance of which the orientation of a man's life depends?

The invitation is not thought of as offered because of any extraordinary psychic experience. True, there must be an inward correspondence to the outward signs of the call. But the invitation is given by outward, objective indications, by the plain teaching of the Church, the reading of the Gospel, the advice of those persons who best know a man's character. The personal requirements are visible and measurable, such as health, solidity and force of character, ability to harmonize with others, good moral traits and record, and aptitude for the studies required— or, in the case of the lay (non-clerical) Religious, for the practical domestic tasks involved. From the standpoint of pure *subjectivism* nothing can be learned.

Nor is it due to any conscious merit on the individual's part. He regards himself as no better nor worse than anyone else. Thousands better than he lack such an invitation; they have their own calls, it may be, which they may follow with varying loyalty and success.

He is simply one of the crowd. He conceives himself as mingling in the varied crowd of saints and sinners on the highway of life. He is neither a priest nor a Levite: indifferently a Jew, Samaritan or Gentile. He looks on himself as one of the less wealthy sort of fellows; looking perhaps for a job; with home ties and home loves, yet out in the world seeking opportunity and adventure. There is a touch of shame for his betrayals of self even in so short a time, and some head-hanging for his foolishness, but yet high hope and great trust in the Father of Mercy has not been abandoned by him.

The more he is one of the crowd, the less he feels himself a man of destiny; the less he is marked out as singular, by religious exaltation, the better he fits into the scene.

He is his own man, with his own personality, his own give and take, and his kit-bag full of mother-wit and a few precious nuggets that Dame Nature has let him stumble upon—which he is always ready to share with his comrades on the road.

Christ, the Divine Carpenter of Nazareth, he meets with casually; as one wayfarer meets with another; on the road, jostled by the passer-by; unknown, almost unknowable. He meets with the Son of Man not in His Divine splendors. Nor does he meet with Him even robed in His earthly dignities as a revered Teacher, Rabbi, and Founder of a Religion. He meets with Him in the simplicity of His family life, in the company of Mary and Joseph, His Mother and His Foster-Father, and the actual dignity of the Divine Personality is humanly garbed, so to speak, in the reverence and deference shown to those whom filially He looks up to as His parents.

Nor is the invitation necessarily extended in one supreme, take-it-or-leave-it, moment of choice. Christ is
not met with thus merely once. He may have been met
with so many times, perhaps daily, over a period of time.
The invitation may have come progressively, by an increasing realization of what the example and the presence
of Christ meant *for him:* by seeing too what it has meant
for others—by reflection on a word spoken by the Divine
Friend, or a comparison, or a hint from Mary or Joseph.

So with the Apostles:—for some, as St. Matthew, in
one supreme command and acceptance;—for others, as
the fishermen of Galilee, gradually, in an increasing realization.

The invitation itself, too, the opportunity extended, is
equally simple, almost casual. It is not the proposal of
an elaborate discipleship. It is not the proposal to be
initiated into a profound, esoteric philosophy: to become
an adept, a master-craftsman, or an illuminate. There is
no portal to pass through into a mystic initiation; no pass-
word to be breathed in mystery, no veiled symbols to be
learned, or sacred rite to be acquired, or high-sounding
scale of degrees to be trod upon.

All that is asked in order to obtain this fulness of
life is that the young man decide to share Christ's enterprise on earth, by sharing in the conditions of His earthly

13356

life. This may seem for the twentieth-century mind to contain elements of the fantastic. To share the condition of life of George Washington or Dr. Samuel Johnson would seem impossible enough at the present day: their clothes, their food, their actual social habits and environment. To live in any way approaching the actual method of life and action of Christ seems the height of fantasy. Hence there is need of a definite explanation.

It is not a question of assimilation in a haphazard manner to the various accidental details of His life, as affected by the social customs which He shared, or the circumstances of His epoch. Nobody but an eccentric would wish to don a Jewish garb of the Augustan era, or live on dates and figs, or wear sandals, or progress from village to village preaching in parables. In point of fact such an accidental assimilation would not in reality be any "following of Christ" at all, since Christ only adopted them in order to conform to the conditions of *His* epoch of visible, earthly ministry, as an example that His followers need to conform to the conditions in which they find *their* ministry, as His disciples, placed.

The question which is the heart of the proposal is that of sharing (by a lifelong consecration of one's entire self) the conditions of Christ's earthly life in so far as they affect all times and all places, as they affect the perpetual and fundamental needs of humanity, and thus being free in heart, mind and body to devote oneself to the Saviour's own work of giving glory and honor to God, and of laboring for the perfection and salvation of one's neighbor.

These conditions are those which Christ asked His Apostles and the disciples associated with Him in His earthly ministry to share from their own free choice, namely, Poverty, Chastity, and Obedience. These conditions He had personally adopted from the beginning of His life on earth. Through them a definite stamp was given to His own domestic life, which He led for thirty years before entering upon public activities.

Once accepted, however, this invitation, which is freely offered to all men, becomes a special gift of God for the individual. This gift is known as a Religious vocation, and, in the particular case here considered, as a vocation to the Jesuit life. "Religious vocation," to quote a well-known writer (Vermeersch, Religious and Ecclesiastical Vocation, p. 49), "is the special gift of those who, in the Church of God, follow the Evangelical Counsels—Poverty, Chastity and Obedience—with the proper intention." It is a gift which is not confined merely to the passing period of invitation, but which lasts throughout life and into eternity. In it are included all those interior and exterior helps and graces which have enabled a man to form and carry out his initial resolution of following Christ in the path of the Counsels. So that included in the idea of a Religious vocation are not only the internal lights and impulses given by the Holy Spirit, but such matters as the gift of Catholic parents, the example of companions, preservation from moral corruption, mental and physical fitness for the duties of the Religious life, sound education, etc., as well as a special aptitude of disposition and character, in this particular instance, for the wide field of apostolic endeavor and the long period of thorough training and grounding which characterize the Society of Jesus.

In the Religious vocation, too, are included all those graces which throughout a lifetime enable a man to persevere in the state of life which he has entered upon. Like the gift of faith, the vocation may be rejected when first offered, or, once accepted, it may be weakened or even lost by neglect of those graces which are given for its fulfilment. The instances of such losses strew the history of the Church. Perseverance therein depends on the faithfulness with which a man keeps the rules of his state of life, and it is often the custody or the neglect of the smallest and easiest prescriptions which determine the loss or the preservation of the whole.

Christ speaks to the young man in terms of Divine

faith. For there is no intention not drawn from faith, no matter how cunningly conceived in terms of self-interest or worldly advancement, which can serve either to win or to keep the gift of a vocation. But given this right intention, and given the aptitude to follow the Divine call, no man need doubt that God will remain faithful to him with His assistance if he on his part is faithful to his first resolves. "Religion," says St. Thomas Aquinas (II.IIae, qu. 189, art. 10), speaking of the Religious vocation, "is the mild yoke of Christ. . . . To those indeed who take this mild yoke upon themselves He promises the refreshment of the Divine fruition and the eternal rest of their souls." Just what the yoke of the Counsels implies is the subject matter of the next two chapters.

CHAPTER II

Spiritual Freedom

I

Why be poor, chaste and obedient, rather than rich, pleasure-loving, and free to do your own sweet will?

There is a chill in the sound of those words. Why *be* poor? Still more, why *wish* to be poor? Why plan to be poor, why love to be poor and dance and sing about it, as did St. Francis of Assisi?

Is there anything particularly noble in squeezing like a criminal through a subway turnstile, instead of having the family chauffeur place the rug on your knees, as you sink into the rear seat of your limousine? Poverty is a nuisance. It loses you friends, spoils your credit, hampers your business, makes the police suspicious, haunts your sleep, puts a sheen on your winter coat, leaves gaps in your shoe-soles, provokes the doctor, and ruins your health.

Chastity is crippling, says the latest professorial pundit. Without divorce-courts journalism would suffer. If your heart of flesh has no forbidden thrills in youth what kind of a past will you have to gloat over when you are old, and bald, and beginning to subscribe to the Life Extension Institute?

As to obedience, what is the use of doing anything if you cannot do what you want? No one knows what you want but yourself, and another man's meat is your poison. Was not Moses disobedient to the King of Egypt? Did he not go down into Egypt Land, says the famous song, and say to old Pharaoh, "Let my people go!" and threaten all the plagues from mice to grasshoppers if his demands were thwarted?

But, and here is the rub, Moses, though defiant to Pharaoh, was obedient to God, and his defiance of Pharaoh was based on a higher allegiance. The path to freedom was through separation and self-denial. Possessions must be left behind: sheep, lands, homes, booths and change-tables in Egypt; and the long road taken into the desert, where fare was scant, joys were rare, and the specter of loneliness hovered above the desolate rocks. For what? For freedom; not of Israel's body alone, for after all there were compensations in Goshen, but of her soul, her nationality, her religion and her destiny.

In exitu Israel de Egypto, sings the choir as the nun leaves the symbols of a worldly career, in the convent chapel at her renunciation, to be clothed in the garments of her new life. The Vows are no softer in themselves than the cliffs of Sinai. They are no more jocund for flesh, blood and temper than the desert dunes. But they are the pathway to spiritual freedom.

A man does not take vows because he is disappointed in love, or because the varnish has worn off the tin soldiers that the world gave him to be amused with. He is not goaded to vows by spite, or floated into them by sweet melancholy. But they lift off the things that weigh down his spirit, and set free the might of his will to embrace that fulness of life which is promised him by the Redeemer.

In the concept of Ignatius, a man's spirit, if set free, will then be guided by the Holy Ghost, the Spirit of love. Instead of raising himself up painfully by a ponderous code of dead precepts, a new law will build up a new life within him; "the interior law of that charity and love, which the Holy Ghost is wont to write and print upon the heart." So in his Spiritual Exercises there is no elaborate code of maxims, inscribed in lacquer, wrapped in blue silk, and incensed each year by bowing disciples. There is but one concern proposed during the time of Retreat, that of freeing oneself from those things, within or without, which most fetter the spirit, that when once the soul is freed, the Holy Spirit may do His work, by recalling and imparting to the soul the supereminent knowledge of Jesus Christ.

The Vows, however, are understood as the most complete, the most effective means to rid the soul of those hindrances from which all men must free themselves to a greater or lesser extent: attachment to material goods, attachment to the satisfactions of the sensual or lower nature, and attachment to one's own supposed excellence, or pride.

In succinct definition, a vow is a free and deliberate promise made to God to perform a possible and higher good. The subject matter of the vow must not only be something possible of fulfilment, but it must be a *bonum melius*, something which is better than its non-performance, or something which does not impede or nullify a higher or better good.

II

"Blessed are the poor in spirit, for theirs is the kingdom of Heaven." Poverty of spirit was never more needed than today. The scandals of law-breaking are but a symptom: misused Government property, bribed jurors, padded payrolls, bribed electors, etc. But the viewpoint, the estimation of all life's values from the angle of acquisition and possession, casts silken threads over the soul, and the spirit is in leading-strings to matter.

Poverty of spirit is not for one class alone. All Christians must practice it in greater or lesser degree. Else no amount of godliness can keep the rich man's waist-line from sticking in the needle's eye. Greater for some, or less for others, it depends on circumstances and vocations in life. Occasions, crises must be met, and the choice made between spiritual slavery and spiritual freedom.

Where, then, does the Vow, the practice of Religious Poverty, come in? When it is a question not simply of keeping the material from dominating when a decisive occasion arises, but of making poverty of spirit the basis, the constitution of life, so that all occasions, and crises, and individual choices are forestalled, their very supposition swept away, by an entire orientation of a man's whole relation to the world.

The manager takes you over his salesrooms, slips the glossy price list into your pocket, points out his glittering machines amid palms, and rugs, and soft, yellow-shaded lamps.

"Our policy," he remarks, "is to render service to the public. We do not wait for occasions, special needs, to show this. It is our platform, the first article in our constitution. We are committed to it, positively, irrevocably."

With a certain analogy, then, Religious Poverty *commits* a man to being poor in spirit. His life is built and arranged to that end. The more permanent and all-embracing his vow, the more absolute is his commitment. Taking the salesman's words at their face value, as meaning a genuine spirit of service, we may point out that sometimes the local garage man shows the same spirit of service. Yet he is not committed to such a spirit irrevocably. He reserves a right to act otherwise, say, when called up at 3 A. M. So an immense heroic poverty of spirit is practiced by countless Christians who have no Religious Vows. In the individual instance they may surpass the acts of the Religious as individual instances. But they are not *committed* to that spiritual poverty, by an irrevocable, lifelong adoption of separation from material personal ownership and personal use. The essence of the Vow is in that commitment accepted by the Church, and the essence of Religious observance is in the fulfilment of that commitment of a man in daily life.

He is committed to a state of life which of its nature (*i. e.*, if he lives up to it), separates him from a bondage which is dear to its slaves, which benumbs modern thought, science, morals and education, and which every Christian must contend with in life and in death.

So in like manner a man can be chaste without the Vow of Chastity, he may practice a certain manner of obedience, without being bound by Obedience to any

Superior save those by law appointed. His spiritual freedom will be decided in each given instance, each of which has its own history, but involves no further commitment for the whole of life.

"Blessed are the clean of heart, for they shall see God." The virtue of chastity, considered in its ultimate meaning, is simply the truth translated into practice. It is that "doing of the truth," spoken of by St. Paul, which is the opposite of a life which, no matter how excused, how painted or palliated, is but a falsehood in practice. The forms of chastity that correspond to the different states of life, the married state, that of youth and maidenhood, widowhood, the priestly state and of lay celibacy—all are simply the expression of the *truth* of each of those states. Just as a house is built true when it corresponds to the architect's plan, so a man's life is built true when it follows the plan of the Creator. God, however, has planned the human body to be used not as an instrument of wilful desire, but as an instrument of His honor and glory. Moreover, in the plan of God, the Holy Spirit dwelling in man sanctifies his soul, gives it its rightful power over the lower appetites, and makes of the body itself the temple of the Holy Ghost. Chastity is simply carrying out in human conduct the vision of the truth seen in the holiness of God, the sole author of all purity.

Evangelical chastity, by which a man, besides observing the requirements of the natural law, renounces his natural rights over his own body and consecrates himself to a life of celibacy, is a state of life patterned on the life of the Son of Man Himself, who wished His most intimate disciples to be not only unencumbered by external goods, but also to be free from solicitude about their families.

"Learn of Me, for I am meek and humble of heart, and you shall find rest to your souls." Obedience is the tool by which meekness and humility are fashioned. Meekness is spiritual power, humility is freedom from the illusion, the contradictions, the appalling weakness, the latent insanity of pride.

Moreover, obedience, in matters which are merely of counsel and free choice, cannot be exercised without some preexisting bond of obligation to obey. There must be someone with the power to command, if obedience is to exist. This in turn supposes a free subjection of oneself to a Superior, and, if this subjection is to continue, it must have a perpetual source in some permanent bond of obligation. A lasting bond of obligation, arising from vows which are made to God, is of the essence of the Religious state.

By the *vows* therefore of Obedience and Chastity this truth of life, these spiritual tools for spiritual freedom, are embraced once and for all, not in single instances, but by one supreme act of interior worship, of complete self-oblation. *Ecce hæc sunt instrumenta artis spiritualis,* says the Rule of St. Benedict: "Behold these are the tools of the spiritual craft, which, if they be constantly employed day and night, and given back in the day of judgment, will gain for us from the Lord that reward which He Himself hath promised."

The priest who vows Chastity, the Religious man who vows both Chastity and Obedience, strikes through the whole web of such individual choices or crises with one blow. He is enrolled, enlisted in the army of those who are committed voluntarily to a state of life which, by its very constitution (if it is lived up to, and the spiritual tools used which it provides), infallibly brings purity of heart and humility of spirit, and thereby frees man by its very supposition from two of the chief forms of spiritual slavery. He places himself under a special obligation. The obligation of fulfilling the matter promised in a vow arises from the virtue of religion, that is to say from the honor and worship due to God, as our Creator and Lord. The extent, however, of this obligation depends on the subject matter of the vow, and the intention of the person who makes it. It may be likened to a law which the maker of a vow imposes upon himself.

Over and above the good that lies in his particular act, there is the special point that his act is the fulfilment of a solemn engagement. For when a man pledges himself, at whatever cost, to render to you always a special service or devotion, everything which he does takes on a special value from his pledge, *if* he carries it out. So with the Vows. Their value for the individual depends upon their fulfilment.

But how are they to be fulfilled? Not by dreaming and looking at the lotus flower, but by intensive and united effort, in some established way of life. By means of the Vows a man actually gives and delivers his own person to God. This is only then effected when these vows are accepted in the name of God, by God's Church. By this self-delivery, with its corresponding acceptance by the Church, a man enters upon a stable form of life: he enters the *Religious state*, which is embodied concretely in the form of a Religious family.

III

When men unite in a Religious family, to carry out the Counsels of Poverty, Chastity and Obedience, they follow no haphazard scheme. Their way of life is a tradition, taken from the life and teachings of a Founder, who derived his prophetic message from the study and the actual *living* of the Gospel. For unless the seed of the Religious Order has been planted by a true prophet with boundless patience, meekness, charity and courage, in a word, with heroic sanctity, it will never grow into a lasting tradition.

We find in the Church not only a variety of Religious families as such, but a variety of Rules and traditions as to Religious observance, all of which go back to the seed planted by the original Founder. I say seed, because not only the Founder's own personal aims, but even the Rule and the working traditions which he established in his life-time do not represent the full tradition of the body as it will be matured by age and experience. Future years, with their future demands for interpretation and ever-broaden-ing action, under the guidance of the Holy Spirit, bring out the hidden possibilities of the original Foundation on which all later developments are built.

The Jesuit Order, or the Society of Jesus, is simply one of these many Religious families which form part of the texture of the Church. Its Founder was a Saint, who in his own life interpreted the Gospel Counsels that he recommended to others. Profiting by the experience of other Orders before him, and considering our tendency to unclear thinking and hazy enthusiasm, he was explicit in the drafting of the legislative framework of his Order, and established certain settled traditions as to their interpretation. Nevertheless, neither Constitutions nor tradition were meant to contradict future progress, but rather to serve as a basis for a future development of sanctity and zeal. This development instead of minimizing the written prescriptions would serve to establish them, and to unfold their hidden wisdom and timeliness.

There is a tradition, a family spirit, very much as in certain families there is a standing devotion to the Army or the Navy, certain traditions of art, or of craftsmanship, or of unselfish devotion to the public welfare. Hence, though certain norms or principles may be set down in writing, though they may be reduced to a sort of family legislation, the actual concrete observance is less a matter of a methodical adjustment to a difficult rule and more a falling in with the ways and traditions of a great and ancient family, itself only a small part of an immensely greater and much more ancient family, the entire body of Religious observance of the Catholic Church. In this great complexus of family tradition, one cannot readily detach what is of one Order or of another. Simple practices that seem quite casual are found to link up through centuries of tradition to the earliest beginnings of Christian Religious observance in the cloisters of Subiaco, or the caves of the Thebaid itself.

IV

The Jesuit conceives the practice of Poverty as consisting essentially in the absence not only of all ownership of material goods—real and mobile estate, personal effect, money, etc.—but also in the absence of all independent use of such goods. Since total relinquishment of all ownership can take place only gradually, and with certain conditions, the reality of the offering is preserved by this absence of independent use not only of one's own goods, up to the time of total relinquishment, but of any material goods whatsoever, including such goods as belong to the community as a body. It is in the extreme dependence experienced in the usage of even the smallest articles of a material nature that the strictness of the Jesuit observance of Poverty consists.

Precisely in this point does his voluntary Poverty profoundly differ from the condition of the merely indigent person. Even if a man has only a barrel to live in, he nevertheless retains some control, some freedom in the use of the little the barrel contains. His appreciation of this independence often increases as its object is less. But the Jesuit controls nothing as his own. Whatever is needed for his life and work is provided for him by the Religious family: clothes, food, lodging, books, apparatus, etc. But in all things he is dependent on the permission of the Superior, even for things as small as street-car fare and postage stamps. Hence between the observance of Poverty and the observance of Obedience there is often little practical distinction.

The vow of Chastity is not understood by the Jesuit in any different sense from that of other Religious orders, or from the celibate clergy of the Catholic Church. The practice of chastity is understood as extending not only to a man's exterior life and conduct, but to his interior life as well, in so far as that interior life is controlled and controllable by the effort of his own will. What is distinctive, however, in the Jesuit conception is the explicit care taken to establish a family tradition of idealistic thought, and of self-controlled behavior, of such a nature as to enable a man to control both his exterior acts and his interior thought-world with ease and complete self-mastery.

I say tradition in addition to rules or prescriptions. For though the Jesuit has at hand written Constitutions that concern these points of voluntary mental attitude and of self-controlled behavior, they are not fully understood without the practice of that flexible and living tradition by which alone so intimate and personal a matter as Chastity can be realized. There are prescriptions touching on self-restraint in food, drink, conversation, clothing, and general behavior. Cautions are offered concerning conversation with various classes of persons. Situations are pointed out which if unnoticed will take off his guard even a man who has this particular observance wholly at heart. Yet without the actual living tradition the words cannot convey their correct import. For it is not only a question of the meaning attached in practice to word and phrase which may allude to still older traditional concepts. There is also a valuation of the important and essential, as contrasted with warnings, or counsels, or mere suggestions of higher things.

The written Constitution is a living tradition of a living family. Just so any great family has its own traditions of breeding, of chivalry, courtesy and honor. It may have its own written reminders of these traditions. They require, however, demonstration, and become awkward when explicitly detailed. Even for us, who think we observe just the right way of holding our knife and fork, there is something clumsy in the same process described, let us say, by a Book of Etiquette. Any Japanese with a sense of the incongruous—as most of them have—can get a most delightful half hour by reading, from the point of view of one brought up on the traditions of the sacred Tea Ceremonial, the precise directions as to inserting a soup spoon into the mouth of Western gentility.

Nevertheless, this written tradition, as expressed in the rules, is the practical test of the sincerity of a man's vocation. Professions without concrete practice are idle. For the rules are for him his guide, the authentic exposition of his ideal, and the subject of daily and practical consideration. Through their observance the vigor of his will, the effectiveness of his actions, instead of being lessened or weakened, is strengthened and intensified, as the stream is kept from dissipation by its channel, as the driving force of the piston requires the firm wall of the cylinder. They have been the tools with which an Aloysius, a Stanislas, a Berchmans and a Claver have hewn a path to the height of sanctity. If he esteems and loves the calling that God has given him, he will esteem and love the concrete means of fulfilling it.

The extent of the obligation of the rules, while it could be exaggerated, so as to give to every individual prescription the binding force of the whole Religious engagement as such, can yet be minimized. For the rules are not mere counsels, once that engagement is assumed. In certain instances they can oblige under sin, even grave sin, according to their subject matter and intention. Even where, as in the majority of instances, no such obligation is concerned, the fulfilment of the rules is not only the concrete test of loyalty to one's supreme life-engagement, it is also the condition for receiving that continued daily and hourly help of God's graces without which neither progress nor perseverance can be expected. With the neglect of the rules, comes the lessening of claim on the Divine help.

Were the rules neglected, mere centrifugal force would drive the distraught Religious family apart in a few years, from the very intensity of its effort and the multiplicity of its undertakings. An active Religious body with neglected rules is self-destructive, for a house divided against itself cannot stand. Growth, continued recruitment of new members, and fruitful endeavor at home and abroad would be impossible were the rules not generally observed, for the simple reason that they are the condition of God's blessing, without which neither growth nor fruitfulness can flourish.

CHAPTER III

Jesuit Obedience

I

If Jesuit Obedience were simply conceived as a mode of strategy—or stratagem—it would enlist no recruits in the modern world. If the power gained by disciplined organization were the prize, it could be won here in the United States by adherence to organizations infinitely less exacting of personal obedience than is the Society of Jesus, and with more *réclame*. Surely if a man is seeking fame and power, or even a sort of collective self-aggrandizement, he is taking a terribly roundabout road to the goal, when he essays to travel thither over the hilly path of religious obedience. The type of men to whom the Jesuit Order appeals are not usually such as are attracted by the notion of another's authority, or by submersion into a collective enterprise, as such.

Obedience has scant attractions either for wilful youth or self-willed age. The notion of an obedient man is not a popular one today. People do not crowd by the thousands to offer bouquets to and shake hands with a man who has performed an Act of Obedience, or, in plainer words, has succeeded in doing just what someone else told him to do. You get into the headlines, into the scenarios, and eventually into the history books by performing Acts of Disobedience and defiance. Hence there must be a super-human attraction, a reason quite above ordinary human calculation, to explain just what moves and attracts men to undertake so laborious, so entirely self-immolating a profession of homage and worship to the Creator. A certain instinct, a certain inborn delicacy of spirit may move a man toward the observance of Chastity. But there is no instinct that moves us to obedience, once we have had but a little experience of what is meant thereby. Man is against the government by his very make-up, and there is as much of a dissenter in the make-up of the Jesuit, by nature, as of all other men. People sometimes speak of the "mystical enthusiasm of obedience," of self-hypnotism, etc. Is the Jesuit Obedience, or indeed Religious observance of any kind, something mystical?

If we mean by mystic a person absorbed in some sort of self-suggestion, captivated by a formula or a certain train of thought, then Religious Obedience is not mystical. A man might put himself to sleep by repeating, *Om mane padme hum;* or he can get his whole world-view shunted off at a tangent from common sense by declamation on

Capitalism, Revolution, Imperialism, Persecution and
Class Warfare.

But no hypnotic state will furnish a man with peace
and strength for a long life of unexciting labor, known
only to God and esteemed only by Him. Such "enthusiasm," in the ancient sense, will not enable him to teach
a class in Greek fifty years consecutively, or help him to
step down with good grace from being president of a university to begin hearing confessions for the rest of his life
in a hospital ward.

But if we mean that Obedience is *supernatural* in its
character, then it may be called mystical, though this is a
loose sense of the word. The motives of Obedience are
drawn from the Faith, and its accomplishment is ensured
by grace, which is a free, supernatural gift of God, without which no man can practice Obedience or any other
kind of virtue. Through the motives of Faith, and
through the action of Divine grace, there is a mysterious
union, mystical in a larger sense, with the obedience of
Jesus Christ, in whose close fellowship the Religious lives,
and with whom He comes in the most intimate contact
through the Sacrament of the Holy Eucharist.

There is only one manner in which Religious Obedience especially Jesuit Obedience can be understood, and
that is as founded in concept on the obedience of Christ

Himself; that obedience which He practised toward His Mother and Foster Father, Mary and Joseph, and toward His Heavenly Father. He was obedient, even unto the death of the Cross. "Going down, He was subject to them." The Jesuit concept of Obedience is not an artifice thought out by a clever man, a military organizer, a wise strategist. It comes from meditation on Christ and His life, and has no other source, no other philosophy.

Yet there is also an inner reason, which gives this observance its peculiar logic and reality.

According to Catholic teaching, the disintegration of human life came by disobedience. The first man sinned by disobedience, and by that sin, itself the primal disharmony, came the physical disintegration of death, war, disease, and the moral disintegration of sin and disillusionment. St. Ignatius Loyola, in those fundamental meditations which are the first philosophy of the Jesuit Observance, regards the realization of this truth as a first step towards the moral restoration of the individual. With peculiar penetration, he represents disobedience as a rejection of the ennobling and elevating power of liberty (*nolentes se adjuvare ope libertatis*). On the other hand, the restoration of a man's moral wholeness implies the restoration of that union of mind and will with his Creator, which is manifested by obedience. Just as disobe-

dience to the Creator is thought of as wilful neglect of
true self-expression (self-help—*adjuvare se*), through the
right use of liberty,—as a wilful lowering of self,—so obedience to God is conceived of by Ignatius as a free choice
of self-realization. It is an elevation of self in the true
sense, for the right use of liberty is based on truth.

By chastity a man does the truth in his own body, so
by obedience to God a man "does the truth in charity,"
with his own spirit. By it he grows into the full stature
of spiritual manhood, as shown by the God-man, Jesus
Christ.

The perfection, therefore, the integrity and readiness
of obedience to God is the measure of a man's spiritual
growth. It is the measure of his spiritual manhood. Since
religious obedience is essentially directed to God, it is
plain that the Jesuit has no idea of rendering obedience
to man as man, no matter how able or how ingratiating he
may be. He renders obedience to man solely in order
that he may thereby have the opportunity of rendering
this particular form of homage to God. Man, as his appointed Superior, simply offers him the opportunity to
practise what Christ practised: neither more nor less.
He sees the opportunity, and takes it, for the sake of following Christ, and offering to God the worship which
Christ offered to His Father, and in company and union

with Christ.   For no matter how high the motive, it is repugnant to see man yield his personal sovereignty even to the best of men.   Personal liberty in its true sense is the last thing in the world that a man would wish to abdicate.   Christ, the most obedient of men, was at the same time the most independent.   The office of conscience is supreme, since it concerns an unalterable relation of man to God.   For this very reason the Religious looks with wonder on the facile abdication of personal liberty, the ready yielding to fads and slogans of the average man in the world of today.   The hypnotism of crowd psychology is more apparent to the Religious, who is out of the crowd, than to the multitude who are carried along with the tide, and think that its impulses, carrying them away from the solid bank of human liberty, are products of their own volition.

For this reason the Religious ideal is not a matter of emptying a man's life of liberty, but of so using his liberty as to obtain the opportunity of practising Obedience, itself the freest of free gifts.   A simple instance may make my meaning plain.   A business man joins the National Guard for the sake of profiting by the training given by that particular outfit.   He has no idea of surrendering his powers of volition, his personality, his liberty in any respect whatsoever.   Nevertheless, in enrolling himself in the Guard, he takes upon himself the obligation of obedience to the Manual of Arms, obedience to the regulations of the regiment and to its legitimate officers, *within the limits of their official capacity*, and as clearly set down by the constitutions of the service in general, as well as by their particular organization.

So, too, the Jesuit desires the opportunity of taking part in the corporate life of his chosen Religious family. It is a free choice, to which he freely engages himself after years of mature deliberation. Certainly an American young man, who enters his noviceship after freshman or sophomore years of college, should be able to know his own mind after two years.

He has no more idea of abdicating his personality, as such, than has the candidate for the National Guard. True, the scope of his engagement is far greater, far more personal, and affecting, moreover, his interior life. But on the other hand, the task undertaken is far more universal and essential, the perfect fulfilment of man's destiny in relation to God, and the spread of the Kingdom of Christ on earth. Yet in spite of the whole sphere of man's interior as well as exterior activities the Jesuit's engagement of Obedience is definitely outlined and conditioned by the structure of the Religious family or brotherhood which is the field of the exercise of this particular offering.

The requirements of this structure are not arbitrary. They spring from the very notion of a family whose members unite not to make life difficult for one another, but to assist each other in a common enterprise. Obedience is not an artificial limitation, it is a constructive and positive undertaking.

II

The scope, too, of Obedience is conditioned by the ministerial work of saving and perfecting souls, to which the Religious brotherhood is devoted. The internal structure of the Religious family, as uniting in a common spiritual enterprise, forms the basis of that rational and deliberate obedience which is rendered by a Jesuit to his Superiors. The limitation, this conditioning of obedience by a definite scope, affects the choice of those whom one obeys, the limits of their jurisdiction, and the manner in which they may exercise their juridical powers.

With all reverence to obedience as a virtue, as means of spiritual development, the Jesuit recognizes authority in no man to command him save those who have a right to do so either through Divine or through human law. In the sphere of civil duties he defers to the same authorities as every American citizen. In matters spiritual his relations to the Pope, as Visible Head of the Church, to the Bishops, and to his own Superiors, are defined by the organic constitution of the Church, which even the entire Order acting collectively is powerless to change or modify.

Nor does the internal assent required by Jesuit Obedience militate against this view of constitutional definition and limitation. On the contrary, it flows from its very nature, in utilizing obedience as a means of greater assimilation and union with both the interior and the external life of Christ. The readiness and alacrity with which Obedience is practised ensure its perfection as a virtue, but they do not affect its scope, its essential function in the field of collective and individual human endeavor.

III

How then about the familiar metaphors used in the writings of St. Ignatius to express a great readiness of obedience: obey like a dead body (*sicut cadaver*); like an old man's staff; that I shall see black as white if so defined?

If these metaphors expressed the extent of a Superior's authority they would not only be alarming: they would be absurd. No man could yield to another human being the unlimited sway that he holds over his own walking-stick. These phrases, however, though vigorously expressed are mere subjective devices to help a man in carrying out a difficult command, which he sees as legitimate and desirable, but concerning which he feels a certain repugnance. They are not to add to the Superior's authority, which is strictly limited by the Constitution, but to help the individual to bring his unreasoning inclinations in line with what his conscience tells him is right to do.

In such a manner one may resolve to obey the alarm clock by rolling out of bed like a log, or obey the signals in football by leaping up like a spring. It is the simple principle of your better self telling your lower self to face courageously what it naturally shrinks from; as on a frosty morning you persuade yourself that the Daily Dozen really is a delight.

But no matter how carefully the extent of Obedience may be defined, the exercise of authority without a living tradition will tend toward formalism. Here again, as in the case of Poverty and Chastity, the tradition of the Religious family is the ultimate factor in determining the application of the general observance to the individual member. Lest there be mistake as to what the tradition should be, the Constitutions prescribe as a basis that the exercise of authority in the Society should be paternal. The Superior should exercise his authority in the manner not of an official, but of the father of a family, with all that is thereby implied of disinterestedness, patience, consideration of human weakness, encouragement of effort, foresight and genuine love for those that are submitted to his care. The Constitutions of the Society, the directions and admonitions given to Superiors insist on this point as on few others.

Yet again the paternal character of Obedience relates only to the manner of the exercise of Religious authority. The father of any American family has much greater scope of jurisdiction over his boys and girls than any Jesuit Superior has over his subjects during his brief term of office.

True, many parents seem to neglect their right in this matter. There are, however, plenty of them who do exercise it, and whether they exercise their powers or not, they possess them from God. The last word in the family is what papa and mamma see fit, and the lawful answer to disobedience is short rations or the end of a switch. The last word in Jesuit Obedience is not what this or that Superior personally sees fit, even if he is wiser than Ethan the Ezrahite. There is but one "last word." It is the written Constitution of the Society. No matter what the provocation, the Superior cannot take any action or make any reply to disobedience save in such manner as is prescribed and provided for in the publicly known laws of the Society.

Within the limits allowed to the Society by the Canon

Law of the Church, the Jesuit's obedience is still more restricted by the limited functions assigned to various kinds of Superiors, as in any workable organization. The law of God, the law of the Church, and the just law of the State each imposes very decided limits within which the Religious observance of the Order can function. The duties of good citizenship, of American patriotism, of service to one's country in peace and in war are observed by the Jesuit as they are observed by all other American citizens in good standing. Moreover, that spirit of alacrity in service, which is held up by the Religious as his ideal in his inner, spiritual life, is his ideal also as regarding his relations to his country, and the practical instances of such willing, unquesting service of Religious men to their country, whether on the battlefield, in the hospital, or in sharing the duties of peaceful citizenship, are so numerous as to require no elaboration.

Nor can a Superior interfere with personal habits and preferences, as long as these in no way affect the spiritual traditions and common life of the Order. In a word, no man is more definitely conscious of his liberties, the Magna Charta of his Christian manhood, as well as of his duties than is the Religious. He lives not under a despotic or arbitrary tyranny suavely exercised—an iron hand under a velvet glove—but under a constitutional government.

Though in this constitution the duties of the subject are plainly laid down, his liberties, at the same time, are safe-guarded with equal certainty.

The fact, too that Jesuit Obedience is paternal and tra-ditional in its exercise, rather than legalistic and formal, enables a gradation to be made (as in the instance of Pov-erty, and the various observances that are a protection to Chastity) between the strict enforcement of such things as are supremely vital to the Religious life, and those that are less vital, merely suasive, or subject to considerable restriction as to persons, places and occupations.

Allowance is made, as in no military or civil organiza-tion, for the need of representation and explanation, par-ticularly in those cases where complex duties or the inter-ests of third parties are concerned. Allowance, too, is made for a certain latitude in the interpretation of the Superior's mind in unusual circumstances, in order to re-main loyal to the ultimate ideal which both Superior and subject are cooperating to attain.

Hence there is a profound difference of spirit between the exercise of Jesuit Obedience, and the military subordi-nation of the armed forces. The soldier, like the Jesuit, obeys according to the laws and regulations of his organi-zation. But the soldier, unlike the Jesuit, cannot thus oblige his superior officer to listen to representations, nor does he enjoy the same freedom in requesting him to reconsider his decision from the standpoint of wider knowledge.

During the World War, while visiting one of our cruisers, the writer was asked by a young non-Catholic officer, "Haven't you Jesuits a head man in Rome?"

"We have," was the answer. "He is the Superior General of the Order."

"Suppose that head man of yours told you to spy on your own country, what would you do?"

"I should pay no attention to such a suggestion," was the answer, "and if he continued, I should conclude he was misinformed. However the supposition of such an injunction is absurd, for if the Jesuit Order countenanced such a thing, I should neither have joined it in the past nor should I stay in it in the future."

The officer reflected. One more question occurred to him.

"Suppose your Superior were to take you out of your work, and send you to some place where you could do nothing at all, how would you act?"

"I should write him a letter and ask respectfully if he might not consider the circumstances before reaching a definite decision," was the reply.

The officer burst out laughing. "Good Lord, Bill," he

exclaimed to his companion, "where would you and I be if we wrote a letter to the Old Man to reconsider!"

The military character of the Society of Jesus has often been stressed. The well-known prayer of the Church for the Feast of St. Ignatius, and the use of various military metaphors in the meditations of the Spiritual Exercises, are alleged in favor of this view. The military metaphor as applied to the spiritual warfare is as old as the Church, and it was only natural that the originator of the Society should make use of such a familiar illustration, and even adopt a military term of the period, *Compañia,* as a description for his undertaking.

Whatever use, however, might be made of the military metaphor in characterizing the spiritual life of the individual, St. Ignatius was far from imposing a military turn to the Constitutions and government of the Society. Not only were there no Generals and Captains and Colonels, as in the Salvation Army, but Ignatius did not set an example for General Booth even in the adoption of a uniform, the last bit of symbolism that a soldier cares to relinquish. When the wearing of a uniform garb was held to be of the essence of any sort of a Religious Order, Ignatious broke with all precedent in refusing at all costs to require of his members the adoption of any form of Religious habit. The spirit to prevail in the government of this

Society was that of a Religious family, not of an army or a regiment.

A simple comparison may show the difference between the ancient use of a military metaphor for the interior spiritual warfare, and the absence of such militarism in the matter of government and corporate life. The motto of the Benedictine Order is *Pax*. No one accuses St. Benedict or the Benedictines of militarism, yet it is instructive to compare the opening of the Rule of St. Benedict, with the initial paragraph of the Constitutions of St. Ignatius.

St. Benedict

Hearken, O my Son, to the precepts of thy Master . . . To thee, therefore, my words are now addressed, whoever thou art that, renouncing thine own will, dost take up the strong and bright weapon of obedience, in order to fight for the Lord Christ, our true King.

St. Ignatius

Although it be the sovereign wisdom and goodness of God our Creator and Lord, which is to preserve, govern and advance in His Holy service this least Society (Company) of Jesus, as it has vouchsafed to begin the same, and on our part the interior law of charity and love, which the Holy Ghost is accustomed to write and imprint in the hearts of men, is to help thereunto rather than any exterior constitutions; yet, because the sweet disposition of divine Providence requires the cooperation of His creatures, and the Vicar of Christ Our Lord has so appointed, and the examples of Saints and reason itself teach us so in Our Lord, we think it necessary that constitutions should be written, which may help us, according to the spirit of our Institute, to greater progress in the way of God's service upon which we have entered.

When Jesuits have been forced into military service, as in France, in defiance of the exemptions granted to clergymen by every Christian nation, they have done their part fairly and squarely in their country's cause, despite the fact that common citizenship was denied them in recognition of their sacrifices. But the military system in which they functioned, with no small violence to their habits as Religious and priests, was totally different in aim, methods and spirit from their Religious life of spiritual fellowship and cooperation in peaceful labor.

IV

To sum up, Jesuit Obedience is an act of interior, spiritual homage to God, offering Him the highest and best part of our nature, which is our own will and judgment. It is a consecration of human liberty, "not as making liberty a cloak for malice, but as servants of God." This offering is made through the hands of our fellowman, in so far as he is authorized by God's Church to be the occasion of such an offering. The scope within which such a spiritual offering can be made is strictly defined by the Canon Law of the Church and the canonical Constitutions of the Jesuit Order, nor can either Superior or subject rightly pass beyond such limits.

The Superior's action moreover is limited not only by the limited scope of his powers, but by the paternal and charitable spirit which governs their exercise. In turn, the Jesuit's obedience is exercised according to a human and humane discipline of union and fraternal love, not the rigid discipline of organized efficiency.

Were efficiency the goal, there are a thousand business organizations on Broadway or Wabash Avenue which could well surpass the Jesuit Order with their skilled utilization of human efforts. Yet all the skill and all the interlocking of human effort in the world cannot do as much for the cause of the Kingdom of God as an hour of silent labor, done in the humble house of obedience, in the spirit of the House of Nazareth.

For the man of clear and direct views, of level head and stable temperament, the man who can see things in their just proportion, and distinguish between the great and the small things of life, the path of obedience is plain. It is the completion of that work of self-integration, of the fulness of life in the service of God, which is the aim of the Religious profession.

The "renowned simplicity of blind Obedience"—blind, that is to say, to the illusions and delusions, the false fears and unreal perversions of the truth that would distract a man from his personal ideal—builds a man's life none the less upon the glory of the Divine plan, read as the Eternal Truth in the countenance of his Creator.

CHAPTER IV

THE JESUIT APOSTLESHIP

BESIDES certain special traits of Religious observance, noted especially in the case of Obedience, we have seen that, in the mind of its Founder, the Society of Jesus is distinguished from other Religious families by the fact that the entire practice of Religious observance by which men gather together to labor for their own sanctification is itself directed towards the good of souls, towards the spiritual welfare of one's neighbor. By a wonderful harmony of conception, the Jesuit undertakes to work for his neighbor by the practice of his own offering of Religious observance. At the same time, his actual work for his neighbor offers the best opportunity for carrying out the observance itself: *ut totum religionis pondus,* to quote the succinct words of Suarez, *illum* [*finem*] *principaliter respiciat:* that the whole weight of Religious observance should bear towards the goal of the neighbor's spiritual good, not as something added to the life of self-perfection, an afterthought, a work of supererogation, but as the actual essence of the observance.

In all Religious families, however, there is a difference between the broad outlines in which they are conceived by their founder and the more distinctive traits which come as a result of their historical evolution and through the guidance of God's particular Providence in their regard. For no founder, however far-seeing, can prophesy the full plan of God. Hence we see the Benedictine foundations take on a great variety of cultural and spiritual life in the course of centuries, which can be considered as implied, but by no means expressly anticipated, in the original Rule of St. Benedict. We see, for instance, the growth of their social and agricultural mission in Germany, their liturgical development in Rome itself, their influence on civic stability in Northern Italy, as well as their missionary destiny in various lands, and their educational mission in England and English-speaking countries.

The plan of St. Ignatius was remarkably definite. The Order was marked out as distinct and distinctive. Yet once this apostolate was put into effect it developed certain further characteristics which were the unfolding of the original germ in the Founder's mind. Leaving to others the careful task of tracing to their origins all the traits seen in the traditional nature of the Jesuit apostleship, I simply note some essential features of that apostleship as it affects us today, exercised in the modern world.

I

A particular activity is felt as a Jesuit work not so much by its actual nature, as by the spirit which it is undertaken, by the incorporation of the work by Obedience into the collective homage of the Religious family to God, and the collective fellowship of that family with Jesus Christ. So universal then is this scope of the Society that many of the works which are more characteristically taken up by other Orders, or by the diocesan clergy, may in some sense be engaged in by a Jesuit as circumstances demand, while still retaining the peculiar concept and spiritual motive of the Jesuit apostolate: such as prolonged contemplation, austere penance, works of corporal mercy or rude simplicity and manual labor, teaching of elementary schools, etc.

After making, however, all these allowances—which are essential to avoid misconception of the reality and a consequent reproach of being untrue to a distinctive ideal —one may still ask if there be not some phase of the apostolate which in point of fact, and in the main, is looked upon as characteristic of the Society of Jesus. The Benedictines, for instance, with all the latitude of their constitutions, lay stress on the solemn and worthy performance of the Church's liturgy, the *opus Dei;* the Reformed Cistercians, or Trappists, emphasize penance combined with manual labor; the Carthusians and Carmelites lay stress on contemplation; the Friars Preachers, on the regular magistracy of preaching and teaching; the Trinitarians, on the redemption of captives; the Brothers of Mercy, on corporal works of Mercy; the White Fathers, on certain types of Missions, and so on.

To quote the Jesuit Constitutions (Formula of the Institute, Paul III and Julius III, n. 1; P. VII, c. 4, n. 9; P. I, c. 3, n. 1; P. VII, c. 2, n. 1, D, E):

> As for what concerns the ministry itself, the Society devotes itself to spiritual rather than to corporal works of charity, even though it also admits these latter, in so far as permitted by works of spiritual charity and by [the limits of] bodily strength. Although in its zeal the Society embraces all kinds of men, and is ready to seek the spiritual profit of all, nevertheless, in so wide a vineyard of the Lord, it exercises a certain choice of ministries and of persons to be cared for. . . .
>
> In its choice of ministries the Society follows this rule, that it shall seek always the greater service of God and a more universal usefulness, since the more universal a good is, the more Divine is its nature. Hence, other things being equal, it prefers ministries which confer benefit to the greatest number of men for the greatest length of time.

In these words we find stated what we may look upon as the most distinguishing mark of Jesuit activity. They express in somewhat more explicit form the thoughts underlying the well-known motto of the Society: *Ad majorem*

Dei gloriam, "To the greater glory of God." Hence the Society is characterized not by preference shown to any one given form of action, but rather by the choice in every direction of those works, "other things being equal," which will benefit the greatest number of men with the most solid and lasting results.

This principle may be observed as operative in the training given to the young men of the Society itself. Special aptitude and the preparation needed for particular lines of work are taken fully into consideration. Nevertheless throughout the course of classical, philosophical and theological studies, special care is taken to ground thoroughly the candidate for the priesthood in the principles which underly every phase of the apostolate.

Coming then to actual works, we find that this choice of undertakings of a more universal and lasting nature results in a certain trait that may be recognized as characteristic. For want of a better word, we say that it takes on the form, in a new country like ours, of establishing the *outposts* of the Kingdom of God, rather than of administering its settled and established functions. The Jesuit appears especially in the New World as the explorer, the pioneer, or at least the pioneer settler, rather than the citizen who comes to fit into a form of life already established and past the pioneer stage.

That this should result from the idea of seeking the most universal and lasting fields of activity is evident enough. For the more extensive the field, and the more strenuous the attempt made to implant lasting and fundamental principles, the more unusual and difficult are the conditions to be coped with.

From our civic life the pioneer stage is rapidly passing, deeply as that stage has affected our imaginations and our social life as well. But in the Kingdom of God these outposts will be found until the end of the world, owing to the perpetual conflict of the Spirit of God with the spirit of evil; owing too to the immense extension of the Church over the whole world. For the spiritual *civitas*, the city of God, has to be spread by energetic labor, forethought and personal devotion against physical and spiritual obstacles.

The idea of the outpost implies a situation and a method characteristic of pioneering, of scouting and reconnoitering, of chivalry and enterprise. The metaphors under which this concept was formerly pictured may not appeal to the modern man as vividly as they did to the romantic mind of the sixteenth century. The crusading king, the loyal knight have given place to the explorer of the air and the hero of invention and service of mankind. But the situation and the method that corresponds to it are entirely modern, and truer than ever at the present day.

By the outpost then we mean a situation of especial difficulty, a critical situation, where especial resistance and opposition to the good is experienced. It denotes scant comfort and sustenance: the dugout and trenches, not the barracks, the frontier line of the settler, clearing stumps and skinning logs, not the fenced and gardened home. In such a situation a man must create resources to overcome resistance. He cannot fit into an established order.

The special situation, however, has its special requirements of method and make-up in the individual. He needs resoluteness and energy of character; training, that a man may rely on his own resources, and not weep when he has to cook his own breakfast; mobility and readiness for movement and action; detachment from material and personal encumbrances; and, finally, a strong bond of union with the center of operations and with his fellow-pioneers.

There must be discipline and there must be detachment.

Discipline is not simply the training of man along special lines of study and research, or drilling him into specialized aptitudes. The football player must know his signals and the strategy of particular plays. He must know the tricks of the opposing team and the weak and strong points of his rivals. But before all this special coaching he needs to learn certain "fundamentals." There are ways of acting which must become instinctive. Sight, thought, impulse and act must be linked by incessant practice, until the whole man functions as one, and not like an awkward bundle of quarreling units.

So no matter how much special study may be needed for particular situations, the pioneer apostle—teacher, missionary or preacher—needs the "fundamentals" of ascetic training. The practices of the Noviceship are not legalistic forms. Nor are they mysterious rites calculated to lull rebellious senses to sleep and put one into a docile frame of mind. When the young man is told to break off his hour of Greek study to start peeling potatoes, or sent to wash dishes in the infirmary kitchen, it is not simply to inspire him with the fact that he is living under Obedience. A training, a strengthening of mind, imagination and will-fiber is intended; a self-mastery which in later years will not make him the hesitating victim of unexpected trifles —to his own detriment and the disgrace of souls that look to him for guidance. By mastery of petty, unreasoning impulses he is formed to carry out the great life desires of his higher, truer personality.

The situation as herein described applies to certain characteristic features of the modern American world; the methods and individual qualifications with which the situation is to be met are taken into consideration by the modern American Religious and the Jesuit. One thing, I think, ought to be borne in mind that the ideal may be understood. If the qualities mentioned, resoluteness, energy, training, mobility, etc., are emphasized in the Jesuit ideal, it is not from any love or emotional devotion to those qualities as such: of the love of thinking himself energetic, mobile, etc. It is that those qualities correspond to the actual situation, as its remedy. Were the situation to change, the methods and immediate qualities would change, for they are but instruments. In private life few of us set great store by being punctual. It is perhaps a useful, but not a winning trait to be constitutionally unable to miss the 8:17 train. Yet in an emergency, when you know that someone's life depends on your administering the medicine at a certain moment, or when the fate of a regiment depends on the exact timing of an order by the volunteer officer, the duty of punctuality can glow like the spheres, and you set your Waltham watch with the devotion with which you would pledge heart and hand to a bride.

II

The modern situation, as we see it in this country, may be summed up under four heads. Men are forgetful or

ignorant of the truth.   Social and economic disorder com-
bine with physical obstacles to hinder the spread of God's
Kingdom in North America.   A vast world of other races
and tongues lies at our doors, in the West Indies and Far
East, to whom the visible Church and her institutions are
unknown. The Church is also faced with a supreme struggle to ensure the Christian education of youth in the
United States and her possessions.   The principal phases
of the Jesuit apostolate correspond to these four main
phases of the American religious situation.   Their single
consideration affords a bird's-eye view of the field of apostolic endeavor.

The principal truths of faith and morals are easily lost
sight of under the conditions Catholics experience in this
country.   Living in a predominantly non-Catholic environment, there is little to remind them of their rich heritage of the Faith once they are outside of the walls of the
Church.   A deluge of cheap printed matter and cheap
amusement tends to deaden the impressions of the Faith
from mere force of quantity, not to speak of the ever-in-
creasing boldness of attacks on elementary morals and the
very foundations of religion in popular reading matter of
every description.   Hence the need of constant and careful instruction in Catholic faith and morals.   Preaching
and catechetical instruction are works directed to meet

this condition, as well as the writing and publication of instructive books and periodicals, suitable for every condition of life: young and old, simple and cultivated.

Furthermore, with the forgetfulness of these elementary truths comes a still greater ignorance of their application to the complex problems of modern life. As one Catholic publicist has put it (Dr. Joseph Eberle, *Schönere Zukunft,* September 25, 1927):

It is not true that Christian ideas and principles are generally known, that they are as common as blackberries. They are best known when primary matters, or things purely religious and ecclesiastical are concerned. But they are often very little known when it is a question of the effects and the radiations of religious truths into the cultural, literary, historical and sociological field . . . The more the banalities of life tend to drag down and depress men, the more important it is that the starry heavens of the Ideal should shine above them, to guide them, to console them, to give them a source of power and enthusiasm, and the promise of a better future. . . . Ideologies, not recipes for the day, are the power-motors of the world's history.

The interpretation, therefore, of the modern world-situation in the light of Catholic ethical and religious principles is the work of the Catholic publicist. As distinctly an outpost in the world of ideas such an activity is peculiarly appropriate to the Jesuit plan of the apostolate. Moreover, to apply the Christian ideology to the world, as the writer just mentioned would put it, demands a careful grounding in the basic principles of philosophy and theology, which few in this country can afford outside of the priestly state, and for which a long and thorough training in those two branches is necessary. The independence enjoyed by the priestly, especially by the Religious, publicist, which is given by a sure grasp of principles, as well as by freedom from ordinary temporal considerations, offers him a peculiar opportunity to cope with this especial phase of the modern situation.

For such independence of merely human considerations, united with a firm grasp of Christian principles, is the safeguard of commonwealth and of religion in a time of social unrest.

The Catholic Church in the United States has been from the beginning the Church of the poor, not only in name, but in word and deed. In that title she glories, and by that title she is made like her Founder, the poor Laborer of Nazareth. Were she ever to cease to be the Church of the poor, were wealth, not the Faith, to determine the counsels of her leaders, it would be the beginning of the end, as it has been the downfall of the Church in times past.

Unless someone can speak for the poor man and laborer, and for the disadvantaged classes of our society, the future of the Church in the United States is doomed. If her voice were to be silent when Christian justice is violated, when discrimination and oppression are the fate of the weak, and wealth can control not only the social organism, but the organs of public opinion itself, then it is but laying up anger for the day of reckoning.

But who can better speak for the poor, than the man who himself is poor, and who will lose nothing he values personally were the roof burned over his head, and he were turned out to beg? Or who can better voice the condition of those elements in our Republic who suffer by race or origin, than those who have learned to prize humiliations, that they may be "clothed with the same garment and with the livery of their Lord for His love and reverence," and to suffer calumny in silence, that they may seek to imitate and follow Christ, "seeing He is the true way that leads men to life"?

III

Yet public utterance and preaching will have little effect unless there is a deepening of the character of the individual. The wonderful growth of the Laymen's Retreat Movement in recent years in Canada and the United States, following the lead of many of the European countries, shows a widespread feeling that the individual's spiritual life must be deepened. The truths of the Gospel need to be brought home to him not simply as warnings or guide posts, but as the very road on which he is to travel, on which to model his thoughts, his aims, sentiments and conduct of daily, practical affairs. The Spiritual Exercises, which the Society of Jesus has inherited from its Founder, St. Ignatius, provide this direct application of the Gospel to life: they are the program of what may be called the Catholic evangelical movement, in the true sense, without the emotionalism and unreality which that term usually implies. They have also served in some countries to link the life of the priesthood and of various Religious communities of men and women with the Gospel as the source of priestly and Religious observance. Today they are bringing back the Catholic laity, men and women, to the same fountain of living waters of faith and conduct.

The Spiritual Exercises also form the basis of the immense work of parish missions, by which the "Last Things," the great essential truths of human destiny are unfolded not in detail to the individual in quiet reflection and personal contact, as in the Retreats, but in broad outlines preached to the masses. The parish missioner stands right at the outpost against sin, vice and ignorance. In the long hours of the confessional he touches, dissects, diagnoses and heals with the powers given him by Divine grace the intimate wounds of countless souls robbed and left bleeding on the high-road of life, and sets them on their way to their destined greatness as children of God.

IV

To each Religious family in the Church appears to be given a special devotional means of spiritualizing the life of the great masses of the Catholic people. The Carmelites have the Scapular; the Dominicans the Rosary and the Society of the Holy Name; the Franciscans the practices of the Third Order of St. Francis, the Way of the Cross, and devotion to St. Anthony of Padua; the Redemptorists Our Lady of Perpetual Help; the Augustinians Our Lady of Good Counsel and the devotion to St. Rita, and so on. The use of these aids to a realization of supernatural truths, their spread and their preaching, is not confined to the Order with which they are chiefly identified. The Holy Name Society and the devotion of the Rosary are found in Redemptorist or Jesuit parishes as well as in Dominican, etc. So, too, the interpretation of the Spiritual Exercises of St. Ignatius, the giving of laymen's and other forms of Retreats and parish missions is universal in the Church, and is now conducted with abundant fruit by all the Orders as well as by the diocesan clergy. So, too, with the peculiarly Jesuit devotion to the Sacred Heart of the Saviour, and the spread of that devotion through the League of the Sacred Heart and the *Messenger of the Sacred Heart*, its chief organ of propaganda. Devotion to the Sacred Heart, and the spread of that devotion is now universal in the Church, and not confined to Jesuit activity. Apart, however, from the formal recognition given by the Holy See, through special indulgences and other privileges, each Order is conscious of a certain appropriateness and ownership in the case of that particular means of spiritualization which happened, in God's Providence, to be confided first to its members, and which in some way is bound up with its own history.

There is an inner tradition, a warmth of sentiment, an intimate connection with the whole structure of daily observance, felt in the case of the traditional devotional and spiritual practices of each Order. This is amply illustrated in the case of the Dominicans and Franciscans. So, too, for the Jesuit the book of the Spiritual Exercises is bound up with the history, the Constitutions and the rules of his Religious family, with its personal traditions and the entire tradition of its apostolic endeavor, in a way that makes the interpretation or preaching of that book felt as specially his own, while at the same time its use is thrown open to all who can find help therein.

V

Physical and social conditions likewise call for the spirit of the frontiersman, and the explorer for the Kingdom of God. The oldest, the most universal work of the Jesuit, has been and still is the spiritual care of the sick in hospitals, the visiting of prisons, and the instruction of poor, ignorant and abandoned children.

It is a striking fact that practically the first institutions established by St. Ignatius were not primarily educational, nor religious, nor for the purpose of immediate charitable relief, but with a distinct *social* end in view. By establishing homes, where under the care of educated and pious women, wayward girls might be brought back to an honorable place in society, Ignatius showed himself a pioneer in modern sociological endeavor. The tradition of interest in social works and a social outlook has always been a characteristic of the Jesuit ministry.

Besides lifelong consecration to the lonely and self-sacrificing service of the hospitals and prisons, and especial care of the blind and the deaf, the American Jesuits are devoted to the spiritual help of the insane. There are always certain members of the Order whose entire life is given to the task of bringing hope and order into the confusion and despair of those who are beyond the reach

even of the most skilled psychiatrist. The conditions of
the immigrant population in the United States, such as
the Italians in our great cities, the Bohemians scattered
throughout the Western farms, and the Poles found in
farms, mines and factories alike, call for endless pioneering, as well as leadership for the second generation of
immigrant Americans. The oldest Jesuit parishes in the
United States—the missions of Southern Maryland—still
offer to the country missionary many of the rude priva-
tions of pioneer days, as do the scattered outposts in the
Southern States, and the Indian missions of the North-
west. Despite the advantages of auto and electricity, the
missionary in these parts of the United States still has to
struggle with loneliness, storms and bad roads, poverty,
opposition and debt in the attempt to provide his flock
with the elements of ministerial care, or the rudiments of
Catholic education. Owing to the changed times, and the
call for social as well as spiritual remedies, the work for
the Negro race, whether in the rural districts of the South,
or in the congestion of the great cities, is an enterprise of
critical importance, calling on all that a man can give of
patience, enlightenment and zeal. Here again a goodly
share of the burden falls to the Jesuit missionary. Last
but not least there is the work of the foreign missions.

VI

The object of missions is to extend the visible Kingdom of God—to place in all parts of the world the visible means of salvation, such as are embodied in the visible Church, with her buildings, her clergy, Sacraments, and preaching, and her characteristic institutions and activities.   Visible results presuppose visible and tangible methods, hence not mere propaganda, but personal residence and personal service both to communities and individuals.

From its origin the Jesuit Order has made every effort humanly possible to cooperate in the missionary activity of the Church, even at serious inconvenience and danger of detriment to necessary works in regions where religion was already established.   The same spirit and the same effort exists unchanged in our present time and country.   In obedience to the call of the Holy See, American Jesuits have taken up missions in widely scattered parts of the globe.   Their distribution is shown on the next page.

Besides this there are twenty Canadian priests and twelve Brothers employed in the Indian missions of Canada, 31 American priests and 31 Brothers in the Indian missions of the Rocky Mountains and Dakota.

	Catholics	Pagans	Priests	Scholastics	Brothers
Alaska	9,500	29,500	21	—	10
Br. Honduras	26,900	419	23	6	4
Jamaica	40,000	800,000	20	3	2
Patna (India)	6,185	23,000,000	15	5	—
Manila, P. I.	—	—	17	25	2
Mindanao, P. I.	315,025	415,181	10	—	—

Total of American Jesuit Priests now in Foreign Missions, 106; Scholastics, 42; Brothers, 18. Total, all members, 166.

During the year 1926, 1,459 priests, 368 scholastics, and 478 Brothers were employed in the thirty-six foreign missions of the entire Society of Jesus:—a total personnel of 2,305 persons, exclusive of those employed in home missions in various countries, which would bring the number up to about three thousand. In the foreign missions 1,-889,819 baptized Catholics and 229,302 catechumens are under the immediate care of the Jesuit missionaries, in whose allotted territory are also found 1,984,175 heretics and schismatics, and 186,138,042 pagans or Mohammedans. They are assisted by 14,137 catechists (men and women), with 1,039 candidates for the native priesthood studying under their direction. Also under their direction there are in the foreign missions alone 4,743 schools of Christian doctrine, 3,729 elementary schools, 81 professional or technical institutes, 270 superior schools, high schools and colleges, and ten universities, the latter with an enrollment of 4,420 native students.

Looking at the life on any or all these missions from the inside, one may say truly that it is the final test of those Vows which are the life-engagement of the Religious.

The missionary is not only a poor man, but he suffers in all instances some privation, and in the majority of instances great privation of personal needs. Much more trying, however, than any personal wants is the lack of those material aids without which he sees opportunities for good lost forever.

In order that his engagement of priestly and Religious chastity be not infringed, he has to use with more than ordinary fidelity every resource provided for him by the rules and the traditions of the Religious life, since a solitary life and exposure to every possible situation bring their dangers.

Not only is his entire missionary enterprise an act of direct obedience undertaken in response to the call of the supreme authority of the Church, the Holy See, by whom the mission fields and their personnel are designated, but a spirit penetrated with the high ideal that this Vow sets before him is necessary, if his life-work is not to be ruined by pettiness and self-will.

In the popular conception, the missionary's life is pictured as a spectacular life-gesture, which begins and ends with a grand act of courage. That he needs courage, both moral and physical, is plain enough. However, in its actual working, it is a daily fare rather of endless patience, endurance of numberless trifles, quiet acceptance of petty snubs and of situations that seem anything but heroic, and a good solid substratum of plain hard work, all the year round, which is more than ordinarily flavored with monotony.

Above all he needs an infinite reservoir of charity. It is not enough to love the world or the mission-field in the abstract, it has to be loved in the particular, with the rind on, so to speak, and sometimes the rind is not very palatable. The great broad considerations of charity are not what count: it is the application to the individual, in the concrete.

There is a little story told of a former missionary, Father N. N., now living in the Far West, which may help to show this point in a very simple application. Briefly put, it is as follows:

In order to bring Holy Communion to the house of an aged Irish woman, the missionary had to drive ten or twelve miles in a carriage. When he came to leave, after administering Holy Communion, the old lady suspected he was fasting, and insisted on providing his breakfast. Rather than hurt her feelings by refusing her hospitality, the priest accepted the invitation with apparent delight, but much against his natural inclination. She set the table, boiled a cup of tea, and finally discovered one egg, all that she had, in the barnyard. The egg was duly boiled and served and placed with honor before the reverend guest.

Exploration of the egg revealed its historical existence for at least a week. There was the choice of grieving the old woman sorely, or of swallowing the egg. The missionary swallowed the egg.

There is no fame or glory in swallowing ancient eggs, but there is charity in a thousand situations of that sort. No man likes to share the Eskimo's blubber in the unspeakable filth of a *khazim,* or sleep in a snow-hut with feet in a pool of water and head next the only opening, or to say Mass stooping over at forty-five degrees, or to wander for months around ice-floes and tundras after a people with no homes, sunken in the most degraded superstition, in the faint hope that a few children may learn a prayer that will be remembered against the incantations of the witch-doctor, or some filthy old men may at least receive Baptism before they die.

Nor does anyone care for loneliness. The rare type of man who is a natural born solitary is a natural born failure, as a rule, in the mission life. It is as hard, if you are dressed in a cassock, to be ten thousand miles away from the United States, in strange climates, amid queer languages, queerer smells, hot suns and assorted creepers and crawlers by day and night, as it is if you are garbed in a palm-beach suit. The memory of home, kindred, country and friends grows rather than lessens with isolation.

For a man who has spent most of his life in the mission field, one memory stands out above all others. It is not the memory of hardships, which, after all, are only a momentary impulse to greater trust in God, and greater compassion for poor mankind. Nor is it the thought of the joy with which God can reward long and patient efforts or the satisfaction of seeing sodden apathy, degradation and despair change to a world of happiness, intelligence and hope. But it is the recollection of the companionship of one's own Religious family: of persons, grown dear by knowledge and experience and mutual forbearance, and of deeds, which can only be understood by those who have labored in common for a common goal.

The greatest privation for the missionary, outside of being reduced to inactivity by sickness, is that of being deprived of the company of his fellows. There is no greater help and satisfaction than such companionship, where God's work permits it to exist, and, as in all other phases of the mission life, that which is granted far out-weighs all that of which one is deprived.

The fact that the mission is a great work does not make a man feel great individually. On the contrary, the missionary feels his weakness, numerically and physi-cally—and morally apart from the help of God—in the face of overwhelming obstacles. Yet with the growth of this sense comes the growth of the sense of responsibility. What you do today will be noticed tomorrow, and the re-sults of tomorrow will determine the loss or the salvation of innumerable souls for generations to come. Were a missionary to realize the full extent of his personal re-sponsibility it would paralyze him. Happily he need but glance at it, as it were, in passing, do his best, and leave all the future to God.

If there is any remnant of "Babbittry" and self-blurbism left in a man, a few months in a leper colony, such as Culion, will remove it from him.

The thought of the Far East, not so much the romance of its boundless past, but the realization that it is the com-ing theater of the greatest events in the world's history, the frontier of all races where the ultimate world problems will be worked out, is a thought to engage a man's imagi-nation. The American Catholic missionary in those coun-tries is at an advantage in the sense that while a representative in his person and training of the Western Hemisphere, he is in a position to enter, by his Faith and by his affiliations, into the spiritual aspirations of the East. And in the end, he will complete that entrance into the spiritual life of the East by entrusting the new, or the reborn Church in those countries to those who have been trained by his efforts to guide their own destinies henceforth.

In whatever field it may be exercised the apostolic work of the Religious is collective, corporate: he labors for his own individual sanctification through the collective effort of the Order for the good of men. The outward eye measures the success or failure of his efforts by visible results, attributed to the individual. But the individual is simply an instrument to carry out the plan of God, which is fulfilled by the endeavor of the Religious family as a whole. The real power and source of efficacy is the combined total of prayer, labor and self-sacrifice, most of which is hidden not only from the general world, but from the members themselves.

The post of honor, then, in the choice of offices and occupations that the Jesuit may look to in his life's work, is not the post that offers the greatest appearance of visible results, of greatest prominence to the individual. The post of honor is that which offers the greatest opportunity of contributing, by hidden prayer, labor and self-sacrifice, to the collective effort of the whole.   Which posts, which occupations offer this opportunity to the greatest degree, depends in a measure on the individual, on the secret tendencies and secret self-conquests which are known only to God.

CHAPTER V

Jesuit Education

No special thoughtfulness is needed on the reader's part to see that the work of education is particularly the work of the outposts of the Kingdom of God. All other activities, all other problems, are reducible sooner or later to a question of education. Moreover, all matters of primary or elementary education depend in their assumptions on higher education, particularly on the work of the colleges. The Catholic college is the very heart of the Church's apostolate. Behind it are ranged all the forces for good, all the courage and loyalty that the Church can muster. Opposed to it is every influence that tends to weaken and dissolve not only religion, but our country, our liberty and our homes.

Apart from the influence of Divine grace, man's accomplishment is determined by character and ideas. Through the Catholic college the characters are formed, and the ideas inculcated, that are effective in God's work on earth.

The American priesthood, on whom the very existence of the Church in our country depends, would itself scarcely exist were it not for the Catholic colleges. Not only do the Catholic institutions of higher learning supply the greater number of our foreign missionaries, but the activity of a large proportion of our missionaries is itself that of higher education.

I

Contemporary opinion frequently represents the matter of the Catholic college as if it were simply an issue between a college where religion is taught, and one where it is ignored. Such a simplification is not quite exact. There is no college in the United States where entire neutrality is maintained in matters of religion, for the reason that no matter pertaining to the ultimate causes of human conduct or even of physical nature can be discussed without bringing in concepts which if not positively religious, at least hinge on religious doctrine. The time has passed when ethical and psychological matters can be considered wholly without respect to religious teaching. That such affairs could be placed in watertight compartments, and discussed with entire religious impartiality, as we examine the mummies in their glass cases, is a mental bubble that experience has pricked. Yet social science, the theory of education itself, economics, even such staid matters as geography and history cannot avoid reference to matters ethical, psychological, and, by implication, matters religious.

To detach, with infinite delicacy, the meat of purely neutral information from the shell of religious or anti-religious implication in which it is offered for consumption, demands a mind with a graduate's training. It is not within the power of the ordinary undergraduate.

Moreover the difficulty of supposing a purely neutral form of teaching is complicated by the fact that anti-religious and materialistic-philosophical theories are dragged head foremost into the presentation of subjects which *do* admit of a neutral presentation. In spite of the vast wealth of his discoveries in the purely experimental field of chemistry, Berthelot found his subject matter too "colorless," to use the phrase of his most recent eulogist, Premier Poincaré of France, and so ventured into the metaphysical, and, by his implications, into the religious field.

Yet the attempt to ignore the philosophical and religious factors which *are* inherent in certain studies only produces dissatisfaction. Such teaching is complained of today as unreal, unhuman, unrelated to life, and so on. It is precisely these implications which excite the curiosity of the present generation of students. The attempt to pass them over is resented as a conspiracy of silence.

Chemistry will be seen in its relation to biology. But biology in turn raises questions of personal morals, of doctrinal matters such as the origin of the human species, and the immortality of the human soul. The extreme complexity of modern life creates a thirst for some guidance out of the maze of conflicting proposals and interests. Studying matters that bear on human conduct and the interplay of human principles, any thoughtful student feels that he has a right to some kind of interpretation of what is going on about him from the teacher of those very subjects.

In other words, the growing spirit of unrest among our American college students is not mere lack of discipline. Some of it comes from dissatisfaction at the evasive answers which are given to these questions which are sure to claim attention when the voice of religion has been stifled.

This ignoring of religion (says Bernard Iddings Bell, bluntly writing in the *Atlantic Monthly* for January, 1927) is fatal to the real purpose of education. Facts and behavior are dead stuff until man begins to interpret them; and that interpretation is bound to become a religious activity. It is religion in colleges that the increasingly rebellious undergraduates miss, even though that is not a phrase that they themselves are wont to use. . . . What is necessary now is an interpretation of science, a restatement of philosophy which shall synthetize observable facts and processes both with man's inner spirit and with essential reality.

There are also further causes of rebellion and unrest, none of which can be ignored. There is dissatisfaction with the subordination of some of our colleges, the natural home of thought and higher ideals, to the interests of big business. There is the suspicion that men are being prepared more for jobs, than for life itself. Financial policies are thought to be substituted for ideas, and teaching dictated by the sway of temporary public sentiment, rather than by calm study and reflection. The great multiplicity of subjects and courses offered to the student is objected to as lacking coordination with any organic idea of the whole purpose of study.

Again, the very method of instruction is criticized. Two points in particular are singled out by the disquieted element for reprobation. One of these is the want of those commanding elements of personal leadership on the part of the teachers whose office it is to present a life-program to live young men. The functionary, the school official are pointed out as being too much in prominence. So, too, the lack of personal contact between professor and student is regretted: of personal, direct cooperation between teacher and pupil, of active, self-sacrificing concern on the teacher's part for the pupil's intellectual progress, of disproportionate concern for material advantages and considerations that affect the good of the institution as such, but are of no immediate concern to the student.   The need too of an international outlook is being more and more emphasized.   World peace, growing from world understanding, is being sought by the co-operation of students in different lands.   The international phases of jurisprudence, of the application of economic laws, of social and humanitarian questions, is brought to the attention not only of specialists, but of educated men. The college student feels he must have more than a polite knowledge of persons and events.   He must be able to see somewhat into the principles that lie behind the scenes.

How far all or any of these criticisms are justified is not the matter of our discussion.   The existence of such dissatisfaction, with the alleging of these and kindred grounds, is an objective fact.   It is also true that the Catholic college takes these points into consideration, and adopts towards them a consistent policy.

As for the work of the Jesuits in the United States, we may say that the educational policy which they have adopted as a result of the traditions of their Order corre-sponds to those wants that are expressed or at least felt by many of the intelligent student youth of this country.

II

The religious teaching of the Catholic college is not a mere emotional frosting on the cake of knowledge.   Nor is it a bit of theological speculation which has been carried down, like a moraine, from some archaic epoch, and is now too heavy to be pried loose from the college campus. Nor is it solely the explanation of the means of salvation, of those doctrines and practices which are indispensable if a complete shipwreck is not to be made of one's career on earth.

The Catholic college goes much further than this. Religion, in its curriculum, is also an interpretation of all else in the field of studies which hinges on human conduct and destiny. It is the interpretation not by this or that clever teacher, whose brilliant sophisms will be mocked at a month after graduation, but of life by the Author of Life, the flow of time by the Eternal Teacher, and of society by Him who is society's end, who foresees the ultimate goal toward which not merely human knowledge, but all creation itself is tending.

Such religious teaching, and the philosophical teaching which is its presupposition and companion, is not only an interpretation of the world as opened to the student's eye. It is also a correlation of the student himself to the world. It gives him not only facts and skills, but it gives him a basis on which he can solve his own problems as he meets them. Instead of setting him adrift on a current to float him to and fro, it sends him out to steer his own boat, or, if we may take liberties with the metaphor, direct the current itself.

The strong character formation and the sense of duty to God and man that comes from religious principle is the best foundation for solid patriotism. The American patriot needs to be more than a flag-waver. The real lover of his country is the man who helps to solve his country's problems because he has found a solution of his own. The record of alumni too numerous to mention shows, that the lessons learned in the chapel and lecture halls of a Catholic college are the best guarantee of devotion and loyalty to one's country in later life.

III

Turning from the general proposal of religious teaching to the specific features of a Jesuit college, we notice especially the *Ratio Studiorum,* or traditional pedagogical method of the Society. The Jesuit Ratio is not an arbitrarily made-up system of rules. It is a selection and grouping of pedagogical methods, in the field of liberal, particularly classical education, which belong to no particular time or epoch. Somewhat as in the case of the Spiritual Exercises, it exists in written form more in the nature of memoranda, to perpetuate a tradition, than in the form of an explicit treatise.

The degree to which a liberal education can be planned according to the principles of the Ratio depends on circumstances, such as the extent that the idea of a liberal, as contrasted with a technical or professional education, is appreciated, the freedom of the college from prescribed governmental systems, or from the demands of other hampering influences.

Apart, however, from its actual operation, the influence of the Ratio as an educational tradition gives a certain tendency to Jesuit teaching, which tendency is patent to one who, like the author, received his college education from non-Jesuit and non-Catholic sources. The Jesuit believes that the four years of college should primarily be not in order to acquire a given number of isolated unrelated facts, nor yet merely to obtain vocational skills as a preparation for lucrative positions in later life, nor yet again to be overloaded ahead of time with the research work more suited to the graduate. His program is the fitting of man for life by a distinctive cultural foundation of intelligence, imagination, self-expression, observation and reasoning power. In other words, he is the champion of a liberal education, as due in justice from the college to those who submit to its mental discipline. He is moreover a believer in using the classics as a vehicle of a liberal education, as a rally-point and means of coordination for all the cultural elements taken up at a given time, rather than a subject of philological study during the undergraduate years.

IV

Besides, however, the specific tool of the Ratio, as an educational instrument for presenting the traditions of our Western culture, there are certain phases of a Catholic college which apply directly to other previously mentioned points of dissatisfaction.

Personal contact and personal concern for the individual pupil is characteristic of a Religious teacher. Since his aim is not a "career," nor a show of outward success, but his own spiritual perfection, expressed in fulfilling his duty to his neighbor, he is placed in a position to command the respect of his pupils not only as scholar, but for his manhood and character as well. His professor's chair is not held in lien to any trusteeship, except to the Church, as the trustee of the Faith delivered to it by Christ. He has actually fewer bonds, visible or concealed, than any form of teacher in modern society, and can express himself with less concern for human respect, with fewer pledges given to purely human obligations. Not only are his mental allegiances known, but their boundaries are known. In dealing with him the student is reckoning with known factors. Once the student has ascertained these factors he is not hampered by personal foibles, nor by elusive considerations of policy, nor by mystic devotion to pet formulæ on the part of the professor.

Passing out from the high-walled cultural garden into the wide plains of science, the study of facts and phenomena, or upon the hills and dales of professional and social study, the Religious teacher frankly recognizes that no collection of facts can be discussed, and no line of research pursued, without reference to assumptions in the field of philosophy. Metaphysics, epistemology, and ethics may be banned with the materialist's book and candle, or clubbed with Goliath's staff, yet the very act of banning or clubbing is itself a philosophical theory, and the hand that wields the club derives its vigor from an implicit syllogism. Here again Jesuit education is seen as essentially the education of progress. Where there is no starting-point, there can be no advance. Beginning, however, from a declaration of those postulates which are inherent in the very expression even of the denial, the teacher of Catholic philosophy measures the progress of the unfolding manifestation of the outer world of nature's laws, the inner world of speculative thought, and the record and motives of human conduct from the standpoint of a definite "world-view." In a word, relations are seen in their proportion because they are related to *something*.

The dissatisfaction that is felt in the present status of American higher education comes, in a measure, from trying to relate everything, the result being that no relation or proportion at all is apprehended, or from trying to relate higher and ideal matters to temporary expediency, the result being that every schoolboy sees the inversion.

When the sea-mist drifts down upon the beach, hiding all distant objects, the sense of size and proportion disappears. A bit of gnarled cedar-bush looks like a tree, a dory hauled up on the runway like an ocean liner, till the wind turns to north, and the fog gives way to the clear, sun-laden breeze. So, too, when the veiling cloud of total relativity is lifted, and a definite ethical or metaphysical teaching is propounded, the world is seen as a structure and not as a teasing illusion of uncertain values.

Because of his definiteness, therefore, in things that are general, the Religious scholar can lend himself to specialties and research with tranquillity and vigorous independence of mind. If such Jesuit research, of the type, let us say, of the Bollandist historians or of Tondorf and Rigge, has not attained a volume in the United States equal to that of the older European countries, it has been largely due to the rapid expansion of Jesuit education in this country absorbing the time and energy of all professors to engage in the more essential work of teaching.

Passing today from extension to intension, the opportunities for certain individuals to devote themselves to special research increase each year, and the speculative field can be more widely developed.

Being separated, moreover, from the great sources of educational endowment, obliged often to struggle with severe material handicaps, the Jesuit scholar works under difficulties that would discourage a lay person, not vowed as he is to a life of detachment.

However much value may be placed on research, the Jesuit Order will nevertheless always consider the office of actual teaching as holding the first place in its educational activities. No office is nobler than that filled by the teacher. No art, however inspired, compares with the art of communicating the truth and of forming human character; and no human science is worthy of greater consecration of mind and talent than the science of intellectual, religious and moral pedagogy. It is a curious comment on our American state of mind that, with our immense enthusiasm for "education" as such, with our readiness to spend unlimited sums on buildings and institutions, the actual *educator* is held in comparatively scant esteem, and we pay the teacher, for whose benefit all this educational machinery is constructed, less, sometimes, than we pay the plumber and the stagehand.

Whether or not he be a man of research, in every case where the Jesuit comes in contact with students, he is primarily an educator. His concern is for the mental and personal welfare of those who have come to college not to admire learned celebrities, nor to listen to exhortations, but to find a way that they can walk, since they see others who have walked it before them.

The Sodality of the Blessed Virgin Mary, as it exists in the Jesuit colleges, is not a mere spiritual adornment. It is an expression of the personal responsibility which the Jesuit educator feels for student life and student character. It also expresses his belief that the development of a student's character must come from within, not as a mere scheme of conduct imposed from without. Such development can only come by inward initiative, based on a man's own conviction, and enforced by his own will.

The hundreds of college Sodalists who receive Holy Communion daily establish the closest contact with Him who is the very source of light and strength in the young man's battle for the good, with Him who is the Way, the Truth, and the Life.

The education of the Catholic college in general and Jesuit education in particular, though it derives from the past those elements which the past has contributed as permanent heritage of our race, looks essentially to the

future. It can afford to wait with a certain patience,
knowing that its principles will gradually prevail by a
process of natural development, in much of the educational world of the coming century. They are based not
on arbitrary rulings, nor on custom or tabu, nor on passing expediency, but on actual psychology, considering the
student not as a numerical unit nor yet as a symbol, but
as a man among men. Though its message is primarily
for the Catholic, it will be found to give a tangible, constructive solution to the vexed question of twentieth-century education, the reconciliation of intellectual authority
with the spirit of inquiry and research, of moral discipline
with the needs of the individual.

CHAPTER VI

Laborare Est Orare

In the preceding chapters we saw the inner aim of the Religious, which is to work out his own sanctification through the observance of the Religious Vows. We saw also the outward activity of the apostolate. To complete the picture the relationship between the two phases of his life, the inner and the outer, should not be passed over.

The Religious life is not organized as a system of philanthropy, or empty altruism. Altruism, devotion to another's interests, flows from devotion to one's own highest interests. It is the result of morals, not the basis of morals. Else we fall into contradictions.

Nor is it organized as a system of efficiency, for efficiency's sake, if such a thing were possible.

The Religious labors directly and primarily for his own sanctification, and in laboring for the good of others he seeks his own highest and truest interests. His direct and primary concern therefore is to fulfil his Vows—the solemn permanent engagement that he has made to God —and to carry out the details of that Observance by which the Vows are made realizable.

For this reason his "success" or his "failure" in the attainment of his ideal is not measured by outward accomplishments, but wholly and entirely by the fulfilment of his engagement to God. This principle leads to a view of life, and of the entire problem of success in life, which is at wide variance with our present-day preoccupation with success and visible accomplishment. Reflection, however, will show that it is a view which leads to profound peace of mind. The peace that comes from the Religious conception of life is not the peace of fatalism or Nirvana, but the tranquillity of an ordered and integrated life, which is the condition of the highest degree of activity and will-power.

For success in the fulfilment of his Religious Observance is always completely attainable. The means are at hand for all, strong and weak, wise and unlearned. Specially notable, however, is the fact that the full accomplishment of the Religious ideal is attained precisely by those things which as a rule are not associated in our minds with brilliant accomplishment. They are the hidden treasures, the way of the Cross, which increases in power with God as it diminishes in the esteem of men. A few instances will show this, and will shed considerable light on the bearings of the Religious life, as actually practised.

I

Humble labor holds the highest place of esteem in the Religious life. It is not a life for dreamers and enthusiasts, but for men or women who are willing to put their hand to the plough, and work patiently, in silence and obscurity. The more humble, the more menial the form that labor takes, the more rapid a path is it to the fulfilment of a man's engagement to God.

"When you work for yourselves," says Bourdaloue, "since you yourselves are small, everything is small which you do; but when you concern yourselves for God, everything that you do has in it something Divine."

Compare from this point of view the life of a Trappist Brother and that of an ordinary farm laborer. Both have approximately the same occupations: to plough the ground, fell trees, take care of the animals. Yet what a difference between them! The farm worker, if he has no Christian spirit, thinks only of earning a living which he will either save or will waste foolishly. The Religious works and suffers in order to purchase the whole world. One is but a mercenary; the other is an apostle and a saviour. One of these goes, with his eyes fixed on the ground like the oxen which he drives; the other looks higher and further, like that monk which a celebrated picture represents as leaning with all his force on the plough handles, while his eyes are raised in ecstasy to contemplate the glories of Heaven. (Abbé H. Morice, *Jeunesse et Idéal*, p. 27.)

The Lay Brother's estate holds therefore a special advantage. It is not a mere plan or "economy," for the sake of securing constant and inexpensive domestic service. The position of the Lay Brother offers to men the highest privileges of the Religious life, without the responsibilities of the priesthood. As a simple proof of the solidity of the Brother's position in the Religious family may be alleged that despite the fact that to the Brother the life of the Order offers less to captivate the imagination than to the priest, the deepest and most penetrating understanding of the Religious life is frequently found among the Brothers, and the most intense love and loyalty to traditions and legislation of their Religious family.

This practical view of the dignity of labor, though based on the concept of the supernatural mission of the Son of Man, offers nevertheless a wonderful contribution toward bridging the distance that sometimes seems to separate the priest from the layman, as well as the manual from the mental worker. In the Religious life priest and layman, student and domestic toiler, are all united not only in one common spiritual ideal, but in one common task of the service of God as rendered by the Religious family. If mere rude labor for its own sake, as told of in the preceding quotation, can be so honored and elevated by the goal of the Religious life, how much more honor is there in that domestic cooperation, which, in the Jesuit plan, is actual part of the priestly ministry?

For, in the Jesuit conception, the members of the community are still more closely united by the fact that the work of the lay members is related to, and is part of the priestly apostolate. The Brother enjoys not only the dignity and merit of Christian labor. He enjoys not only the privilege of the combined service of the whole Religious family. He also takes part in the actual work of the priesthood, with which he is more intimately associated than is possible in other states of life. Without the heavy responsibility or the anxiety of the priesthood or the grievous accounting for talents which must be faced by the scholar and teacher, the Brother quietly, unobtrusively takes his part in the collective homage offered to God, the work of mutual help in the task of self-perfection, the one undivided endeavor for the good of men by which that homage and that self-sanctification are encompassed.

The work of the Brother, from the merely outward view, is one of great responsibility and practical importance. His offices are truly the offices of the family, not the jobs of an employe.

A haphazard review of some Brothers personally known, calls to mind the following occupations held by them in the writer's own Province: Accountant, infirmarian, manager of printing plant, printer, assistant director of College Debt Fund, baker, cook, supervisor of

Province farms, sacristan, secretary of Provincial, church decorator, tailor, porter, college infirmarian, institutional purchaser, custodian of observatory, treasurer, gardener, stenographer, steward.

The possession of knowledge or vocational training over and above the required level of common-school education fits the Brother for the corresponding degree of responsibility.

It takes, however, personal observation to realize how wide and deep can be the influence for good of a Brother who continues in the tranquil fulfilment of some responsible occupation. To take a single instance. The quiet, manly example of Brother Grogan, S.J., sacristan of St. Ignatius' Church in Baltimore, was felt not only by the hundreds of boys whom, as director of the Sanctuary Society, he had trained to reverence, piety, and Christian manners, or by the members of his industrious Thread and Needle Guild, but by numberless parishioners who witnessed year after year the endless pains with which each feast of the Church was prepared for, the calm temper under provocation, the recollection and reverence which grew instead of lessening with continued familiarity with the altar and its surroundings.

Only those who have long been familiar with the life of a Religious community can realize how far-reaching is the influence of a single devoted Brother for the good and the happiness of the group as a whole. But when that work, valuable in itself, is joined to a spirit of faith, it is then lifted into the highest sphere of collective effort, and becomes the type of the life-work of the true apostle and follower of Christ.

On the other hand the priest has ever before him, to humble him and remind him of his accounting before God, the example of the Brother's service. United with him in all the details of his daily family observance, wearing the same kind of garments, eating at the same table, and bound by identical rules, he is one with him in death, and learned and unlearned, scholar and laborer alike, are counted as equal in the prayers and spiritual privileges of the Order.

Instead of the Brother being a sort of practical afterthought, admitted to the fellowship of others through expediency or courtesy, he is in fact the prototype of the Religious. The Priest-Religious is a product of later evolution in Religious life. During the centuries when the Religious life first took definite shape, especially under the Rule of St. Benedict, the majority, in many cases practically all the religious were laymen. Manual toil, not the offices of the ministry, were the occupation of the monk. Even at the present day the life of the Trappist and the Carthusian is the life of the lay-worker. Those among them who happen to be priests, except for the celebration of the Mass and some few limited priestly duties interior to the Monastery, live and work as laymen. St. Francis of Assisi was not a priest, nor were the majority of his early Franciscan companions. Owing to their solid grasp of those matters which are the common philosophy of all Religious life, the Lay Brothers of the different Orders meet with one another on the closest possible ground. They form also the bond of union between the older clerical or priestly Orders and the Congregations composed entirely of lay Religious which exemplify today, by their lives of tremendous fruitfulness and heroic self-sacrifice, a genuine type of the Religious ideal in the Church. Since the actual life of Christ is the charter of the Religious life, one cannot avoid the observation that for thirty years of that life Jesus of Nazareth led the life of the Lay Brother, the life of constant, domestic labor, and only for three years—even these abundantly mingled with humble toil—did He lead the life of the outward, priestly ministry.

II

Sickness and suffering, instead of being handicaps, are recognized in the Religious life as being a generous help towards the sanctification of the individual, provided they are accepted in the right spirit. The Jesuit Constitutions place store on health, as an inestimable gift of God. The Jesuit rules not only bid a man take reasonable measures to preserve his health, but make certain individuals responsible for the health of the community. The Religious life is itself a healthy life. With fewer pleasures, plainer food, and longer hours of work than most men, every Religious community can show abundant examples of healthy, ripe old age.

Sickness, however, say the Jesuit Constitutions, is no less a gift of God than health, as long as it comes from no wilful negligence, and is accepted and patiently endured as a gift. Were the Religious to feel his usefulness ended, his accomplishment ceased, when his outward accomplishment had ceased, great distress of mind would be in store for the sick or disabled man who for his life-time had been wrapt up in the most absorbing of all works, that of laboring for the good of others. The Religious, however, cannot be "shelved" in the common sense of the word. He may vanish from the public eye. His pulpit, his lecture chair, his desk or even his confessional may be abandoned. But his work goes on from the silent battle-field of the sick-bed, until absolutely the last moment of his conscious existence. The disabled, the crippled, the helpless in the Religious community are not its dead liabilities, as they would be for a concern organized for ordinary "efficiency." The Religious family does not present them with a golden loving-cup, a testimonial for services rendered, and then pension them off out of mere charity. Nor are they even like the aged and sick in an ordinary worldly family, to be borne with patiently, as loved ones to whom much is due, with resignation, but a half-concealed wish that somehow the burden may soon be lifted from the living. Even more than the toiler and struggler they are the exemplars of the finest flower of the Religious life. For them the offering is complete. It is the worship of the holocaust, the total burnt-offering, that they render to God. It is the ultimate following of the Crucified, the last and decisive touch in the great life-work of establishing the entire self-integration of their lives, in union with the mind, the will and the love of the Creator. Whatever difficulties the Religious life may present to a man during his life-time, it is the supreme consolation of his old age and infirmity. It offers the most adequate, the most human and all-embracing solution of that ultimate stadium of life, in which the mocker's gibe and the deceiver's promise are both of them stripped of their illusions, and man is face to face with reality.

plete confidence that God's help will be given. But after all proof of sincerity of purpose has been given by a man's wholehearted striving, the actual result, the actual good accomplished, lies with God.

As far as human efforts go, they amount to nothing without the help of God. "So you also, after you shall have done all these things that are commanded you, say: We are unprofitable servants; we have done that which we ought to do." With God is the increase.

Just as the Apostleship draws its power from the inward work of the individual's sanctification of himself, so, to complete the picture, does the Apostleship act as the most powerful means of sanctifying the individual. It is precisely in this *explicit* use of the work for the neighbor's salvation and perfection as the *principal* means for the sanctification of the individual (rather than other practices, as the liturgy, penance, manual labor, etc.) that we distinguish the Jesuit spiritual ideal.

The very elements of the Religious life which assimilate it to the life of Christ, result from sharing in the ministerial work of Christ. Detachment from earthly goods, labor, toil, physical discomfort or suffering, spiritual trials, humiliations and disappointments, the sacrifice of earthly ambitions and the entire consuming of self as a holocaust in the service of God is the part of the missionary, the Religious teacher, the zealous worker of every description in God's Vineyard, as it was of the Redeemer Himself. At the same time that spirit of charity, which is the heart of all Religious observance of whatever kind, is kindled by the task of laboring for others as long as that labor is preserved by some degree of self-denial from the corrupting influence of self-love. For the man who knows how to avoid too much sparing of himself will be the more sparing of others.

Half a century ago there lived in the Maryland Missions a plain old missionary. He was an Italian known neither for learning nor for eloquence, nor for any particular charm of manner. His words as well as his appearance were unimpressive, his methods simple, as they indeed had to be in that place and time. He lived on hard fare, slept wherever he could find a straw bed, bunked over the sacristy on the missions, and spent his days and nights on the road, looking for the poor, the sick and the negligent. When he died, he left an old cassock, a crucifix, and a diary, written in painfully practised English, and in a queer rambling hand, stiff from holding the reins over country roads. It was written only for himself and God, to fix, as it were, his own reflections. He also left a memory, as of a Father of the Poor, in the minds of a few old Negroes still alive at this date of writing. From the Diary

of Father Livy Vigilante I noted the following little re-
mark, without altering his original grammar. I believe it
is applicable to all of us, not to Religious alone. "Zealous apostolic work without bodily and exterior mortifica-
tion hardens the heart more than sanctify it. Constant
experience proves that amply." It was the touch of merci-
lessness to himself, which that particular old missionary
added to what cold and hunger inflicted on him from without, that gave him the touch of mercy to his fellow-man.

IV

Least of all can any man who understands his priestly
office scout the importance placed by the Religious on the
inner life of prayer.

Side by side with Father Vigilante's Diary repose the
memoranda of one of his predecessors, Father James Walton, written some sixty years earlier. Few priests were
more active than Father Walton. The old churches of St.
Inigoes Manor, built in 1780, and of St. Thomas' Manor,
finished in 1798, stand today as records of his zeal. Yet
few men were more contemplative. Thrown entirely on
his own resources, and deprived both of the obligation and
the consolation of being a Religious—for he lived during
the time of the Jesuit Suppression—he found strength,
light and power for his work in the unfailing source of the

inner life.   And studying the history not only of this group of active missionaries, but of all practical workers in God's vineyard besides, the unvarying law is seen that those who in the end accomplish the most lasting results for the Kingdom of God are those whose lives are most deeply rooted in prayer.

Only in proportion to the *inner life* of the individual can he be sanctified by the work of laboring for others. It is just this neglect of the inner life which produces the unwelcome type of the meddlesome philanthropist, the self-seeking "joiner" in fruitless activities, which we see so much of today in our own country.   A strong body is built up by exercise and food.   Food without exercise merely burns up the tissues, and results in decay of vitality.   So an inner life without any observance of zeal, penance and charity burns itself out and degenerates.   On the other hand, exercise without food—valiant outward activity without an inner life to nourish it—leaves one prostrate in the end.   Inward resources are soon exhausted, and the result is in the end a total ruin.   But the hearthstone of the inner life is prayer.   In proportion as the edifice of outward activity and sacrifice is higher and vaster, so must the life of prayer be deeper.   Hence, for the Jesuit, whose plan of apostleship is one that draws as much on human resources as is possible for mortal nature, the deepest and most intense form of prayer is needed if he is to encompass his end. This is mental prayer, or contemplation. The Religious devoted to the active life should be a man of prayer not in spite of his activity, but because of it.

The idea of mental prayer results as naturally from the idea of companionship with Christ as does the idea of Poverty, Obedience or any other form of the Religious life. The outwardly active part of the Apostles' life was only a part of their relationship with the Master. "Mary hath chosen the best part, which shall not be taken from her," said Christ in the house of Bethany. So in recalling their period of visible fellowship with Jesus Christ, the Apostles looked back to the hours of quiet intercourse, when in private and seclusion they listened to His words of instruction, warning and encouragement. They joined with Him in prayer. They asked His advice about the future. To Him they declared their doubts and fears. They conversed with Him informally, openly, together or as individuals. They sought and obtained the guidance of the Holy Spirit that they might recollect His words and understand His lessons after He was no longer visible among them.

So mental prayer, as an actual practice of the Religious life, means the explicit use of a definite part of one's daily time to practise direct, personal intercourse with Jesus Christ, and with our Father in Heaven through Jesus Christ, His Son. It means a freely willed use of one's inner mental, imaginative and volitional resources towards this end. It implies also the inward assistance and guidance of the Holy Spirit, by whom and through whom we raise our hearts and our minds to God. It implies also a certain method or system, without which our efforts are wasted, and apt to end in illusion.

The idea of a certain method or system to be observed in order to practise mental prayer was not a novelty of the Society of Jesus. That the exercise of the soul needs guidance as much as, nay far more than, the exercise of the body is as old as Christianity, to say the least. The spiritual athlete needs training as does the bodily runner or boxer. And like the candidate of the stadium or the track he looks for guidance to men who have already mastered the art. Athletic training is not the supplying of forces to the weak. It is but the direction of forces already acquired or acquirable. So the effort and the power of mental prayer must come from the inner resource of the disciple, as well as from the Spirit of God, who alone can make those efforts and resources fruitful.

What, however, may be considered as more distinctive of St. Ignatius Loyola was that he presented the principles of the contemplative life to men in a simple and, one may say, popular form, after having passed them through the crucible of his own personal experience. As far as possible he freed them of the veil of mysterious allusion and poetic analogy which had made them in earlier centuries difficult of acquisition either by the unlearned or by the active and practical man. He laid down simple rules of interior guidance in a literal and concise form. His work brought the life of prayer home to the modern man, in the shape that the modern man can appreciate, and which has shown itself as adaptable to every variety of temperament.

Freedom from external distraction, recollection of Divine mysteries or of the truths of the Gospel, definite mental and volitional activity, a certain guidance of bodily posture, a rhythmic division of time and effort, a mingling of the vocal with the purely mental forms of prayer, were not inventions of St. Ignatius. They are inherent in the contemplation of all times and of all masters: as proper to St. Anthony of the Desert, to St. Bruno, St. Bernard or St. Gertrude as to the Cave of Manresa.

It may be noted in this connection that of all other Religious bodies, the Carthusian Order showed itself most sympathetic and appreciative of the ideals of St. Ignatius when he first propounded them. With them the Jesuit formed a spiritual fellowship and compact. To them he gave, as to his own companions, the Spiritual Exercises in which his methods of mental prayer are outlined, not so much in any set form of words, but rather in memoranda for a living family tradition. Yet the Carthusian Order is of all Orders of men the most completely given to mystic contemplation, the furthest removed from all appearance of outward activity.

V

One more element remains to complete the picture seen as a whole of the inward and outward ideal of the Priest, as well as of the Religious. This element, that of union with Christ, is the consummation and at the same time the basis of all that has gone before. Precisely here is felt the contrast between the true Christian conception of life, and the peculiar form of exaggerated individualism which had its rise in the spiritual revolt of the sixteenth century.

The shadow over modern life, with all its external glitter and gregariousness, is its inner loneliness. Revolt from the service of God has brought about a desolate isolation of the soul. Outward union, through mass activities, through the hypnotism of absorption in great "causes," brings but a temporary relief. The abandon-

ment of personal self-respect, through sensuality and passion, leading to unchastity, only drives in to the point of
despair the ultimate sense of utter isolation and separation from all that can truly enlarge and expand one's personal littleness, one's personal incompleteness.   For no
one can suffice to himself.

By the inward bond of grace, as the result of the in-
dwelling of the Holy Spirit, the members of the Church of
Christ are united to its Head, Christ Himself.   By reason
of that grace, all their good works, their labor, their daily
occupations, their prayers and sufferings enable them to
realize that union, and intensify and perfect it ever more
and more completely.

So in the Religious life.   Whether we look at the outward or visible efforts of the Religious, his fulfilment of
his Vows, his ministerial or domestic or apostolic activities, or whether we look at his inner life of prayer and
aspiration, all tends to unite him more and more closely
with Christ and more completely.   But union with Christ
brings union with one's brethren through the bonds of fraternal love.   The spirit of fraternal love is the fruit of intercourse with Christ, whether spiritually in prayer, or
sacramentally in the Holy Eucharist.   "By this shall all
men know that ye are My disciples, that ye love one another."   The more a man has striven to attain the ideal

of the Religious life, the more he has thrown himself into its labors, the more he has personally been willing to give of himself for it, the more profoundly does he feel that its inmost spirit is the spirit of love.

This union, however, is not with one who is absent— merely thought of in pious memory, or conceived of as present solely in some transcendental sense. The daily Sacrifice of the Mass is not simply an ornament to the life of a Religious or a priest. It is the center of his daily life. His life is a perpetual companionship with Christ, present upon the altar. Christ actually living with him, under his roof, in the Domestic Chapel of the Religious community, is the object of his daily prayer and contemplation. His daily examination of conscience, his confessions, his vocal prayers, are made with reference to Christ, who is there present.

More than that, his life is a part, an extension, if one may say so, of the Sacrifice of the Cross, which is perpetuated and brought home to us by the daily Sacrifice of the Mass. And since his ministry, his outward activity of teaching, preaching, writing, etc., is one with not only his outward life but his inner life as well, so all his active life as well takes on a certain mystical character. For if done in the right spirit it enables him to take part more worthily in the celebration of the holy Sacrifice, if he is a

priest, or in its participation, if a layman. If we turn
from general ideals to the Jesuit's daily life, we find that
many of the features of the latter are those which will naturally be observed by priests living in common. Common
life itself is expressly recommended by the Church to her
priests, even if they are not members of Religious communities. The private recitation of the Breviary, instead of
the public recitation or chanting in choir of the Divine Office, which is the practice of the older Orders, removes
one of the principal differences which would otherwise exist between the daily program of the Religious or monastic
priest and the non-Religious or secular.

After rising at the time determined by the custom of
each Province of the Society, one visits the Blessed Sacrament in the Domestic Chapel, in order to greet the Saviour
there dwelling in the midst of His brethren, and to renew
pledges and good intentions for the coming day. Each
member of the community then spends an hour of mental
prayer, as a source of spiritual light and strength, and as a
preparation for celebrating the Holy Mass, or for assist-
ing at Mass and receiving Holy Communion. The hour's
meditation is as a rule made privately in one's own room.

This time of quiet communion with the Saviour, of
frank discussion with Him of all personal problems and
needs, of calm and recollected study of His life and of the

mysteries of His love as shown in His dealings with men, and of pleading for His aid in the accomplishment of one's daily task, is, outside of the Holy Mass itself, the most precious part of the day, and the most fruitful for all good for oneself and for one's neighbor.

At breakfast silence is observed, and a brief mental retrospect made of the morning's meditation. At the other meals usually a book is read by a reader appointed for the week, in accordance with the old monastic custom, and the usual Latin graces precede and follow the meal. Conversation at meals is reserved for special feasts of the Church, or other special occasions. After the noon and the evening meal the members of the community spend usually a short time in recreation.

The Blessed Sacrament, reposing in the Domestic Chapel or in the adjoining Church, is visited from time to time during the day, according to custom and the devotion of the individual,—the last visit occurring usually at night just before retiring.

Twice during the day, at noon and at night, fifteen minutes are set aside for the examination of conscience. Each of these periods serves as a renewal of spirit in the midst of the daily stress of occupation and distraction. Gratitude to God is revived in the heart for His continued Providence and goodness, not only in general, but as seen in the events of each day and each hour. Grace is implored for self-knowledge, and freedom from the entangling chain of spiritual forgetfulness or illusion. Transgressions and negligences are checked up and sincerely repented of. Resolutions are made for the future of greater fidelity in the Master's service.

Even if it have no other effect, such a daily examination is needed to preserve in a priest that profound sense of responsibility without which he cannot adequately fulfil the office entrusted to him by the Church. Those who take lightly the idea of frequent self-examination give but scant thought to the accountability which the priest or the candidate for the priesthood has before God in the conduct of his daily life. The pastor, who must render an account of his preaching, his administration of the Sacraments, his care of the sick, the poor and of children, and the management of the temporal goods of the Church,—the teacher, who must pass daily in review his conduct in the guidance and the formation of youth,—the student, who knows that the time of preparation and training given him by God will never return—all realize that no pains can be too great to ensure the just fulfilment of their stewardship.

Through the faithful observance of the "particular examination," by which attention is focused on one's characteristic failings and weaknesses, the earnest warning of the Saviour is heeded, to "watch and pray, lest ye enter into temptation!" For in dealing with self, as in dealing with any problem, the most lasting results are achieved by improving one thing at a time, and by paying attention to the weakest element in the situation.

The recitation of the Litanies of the Blessed Virgin and of the Saints, as night-prayers, sometimes accompanied with Benediction of the Blessed Sacrament, is the only devotional exercise performed daily by all the members of the community in common. Daily reading for a short period of some spiritual book, preparation of the subject matter of the next day's meditation or hour of mental prayer, (before the second examination of conscience), and the private recitation of the Rosary complete the Jesuit's daily program.

As is easily seen, this formal program is simple enough, and there is nothing much to distinguish it from the daily spiritual exercises of any seminarian, or of priests leading a common and more or less regular life. St. Ignatius, however, purposely prescribed that his followers should observe in matters of food, clothing, habitation, etc., the custom of frugal priests of good standing in their respective countries. Their formal spiritual program accordingly was to be simple and flexible, for the very reason that he supposes them to be men of prayer, to be given to interior union with God and a true spirit of recollection which will exist not only during their periods of formal devotion, but will pervade and spiritualize all their work and their entire waking time.

VI

The following brief notes, taken from the short life-description of a Brother well known to the writer, may help to lend more meaning to the preceding discussion. They relate to Brother Theodore Vorbrinck, who had charge of the farm at Woodstock College, the Jesuit scholasticate in Maryland, from 1867 to 1912.

A catalogue of Brother Vorbrinck's doings at Woodstock all these years since 1867 would be monotonous. Striking single incidents there were not, and ostentation about the last thing one would dream of associating with his name. With his plain, matter-of-fact devotion to duty, his unassuming manner and subdued voice, he might easily pass unnoticed for months at a time in the routine life of a large community. Yet when he died, from every one of the simplest acts of duty there seemed to arise a melody of singular charm in praise of God. What less romantic task than setting the breakfast table after the evening meal? But when you reflected that the familiar figure, whose air of serious recollection and quiet diligence fixed your attention, had been thus engaged every evening for almost half a century and when you heard it whispered how, on his own confession, he had that day broken a plate for the first time in forty-four years, you felt that here was something better than romance.

Those who were privileged to see the more intimate personal side of Brother Vorbrinck's life, would be able to say more of his inner sanctity. We, who watched it from without, could only reason to the spirit which prompted these manifestations. We surmised a deep devotion for our Blessed Mother, when on St. Alphonsus' Day, year after year, we always saw him serving the Mass at her altar, and when every morning of the year he might be seen paying his devotions at her grotto. We almost saw St. Joseph in life again as we watched this faithful and prudent servant whom the Lord placed as guardian over a portion of the temporal welfare of His family and who gave us in due season our measure of wheat.   In the true spirit of a Jesuit, his farm was his choir. . . .

No one who came in contact with Brother Vorbrinck could fail to recognize that he was a man of prayer. During his years of active service, it was his duty to see that the farm hands were about their work on time. This necessitated an early breakfast, and the hearing of an early Mass. That his meditation might not suffer, he used to rise earlier than the rest of the community; and when the clock struck four A. M., he might have been seen kneeling in the silent chapel alone with God. This love of prayer was with him to the very last . . . It is a singular testimonial to the length and hiddenness and constancy of his devoted service of the Master, that of all the graves which cluster around the Woodstock Mortuary Chapel—and they are not a few—but two were not dug by his own hands. Around the graveyard and the farm, around the chapel and the grounds around the house itself, there clings the memory and the fragrance of Brother Vorbrinck's life. It was a life spent faithfully and gladly, all for God.

Shortly after the death of Brother Vorbrinck occurred the death of one who had been for several years his Superior at Woodstock.   Father Brett's last utterances, as told by one of his companions, serve too to summarize the thoughts of this chapter.

Just before receiving the Last Sacraments he grasped me by the hand and begged me to accept from him his act of faith in God, in all revelations of Our Lord Jesus Christ and in all the teachings of our Holy Church. He begged me to accept his expression of gratitude for all God had done for him: his birth from Catholic parents, the gift of faith in Baptism, the devotion and good example of these same parents, the advantages of a Catholic education, his vocation, his vows, his priesthood, and the other graces that God had given him. Almost passionately he declared that in me and through me he begged pardon for all offences he had ever given to his fellow men. He regretted and craved indulgence for any unkind word, and above all for any unkind deed he may have done, and asked as a dying man for the forgiveness of all. Then begging God's mercy and pardon for all his offences against His Holy Law, he asked for the Last Sacraments to sanctify and strengthen him on his way.

Life, in St. Gregory's familiar words, is a sort of night-watching for eternity: *est vigilia quædam æternitatis*.

What matter the cold and weariness of the night, if the watcher be found true to his trust when the Master comes in reckoning at the day-break?

CHAPTER VII

THE JESUIT AND THE WORLD

THE best known fact about the Jesuit Order is that it has always met with extraordinary opposition, from powerful individuals, from governments, from elements in the Church itself. There is no need here to recount the numberless instances from the past and present to prove this thesis. Where such opposition is not present, the Jesuit knows it may readily occur, and flare up again unexpectedly at small provocation.

Nor shall we discuss here the many reasons that are alleged in justification of such opposition. They are ably treated by such well-known authors as Duhr, Pollen, Féval, de Ravignan, Lippert.

Keeping to our point, which is simply the characterization of the Jesuit ideals and aims, as patent from the Constitutions and the actual life of the Order, we ask simply, what is the explanation of this opposition from the standpoint of these ideals, from the standpoint of the nature of the Religious life? A few considerations will show that this familiar historical fact is not such a mystery as it may at first sight seem.

128

I

The opposition incurred by the Society is, after all, only a *degree* of the opposition experienced by larger groups of men, of whom the members of this particular body form a part. The definite vowing of oneself to the pursuit of justice runs contrary to the easy-going ways of men.

The Church has always experienced bitter opposition from the world. This opposition was prophesied by Christ Himself in no uncertain terms. "The servant is not greater than his master. If they have persecuted Me, they will also persecute you." Not merely Jesuits, but devoted Christians of every description, and particularly members of all the Religious Orders, have shared in the common lot of the Church in proportion as they showed themselves zealous in upholding or spreading the Kingdom of God.

The root of this general phenomenon of opposition between the Church and the world is in the whole supposition and history of Redemption. It is intensified by the conflict of actual guiding spirits. There is no compromise between the Spirit of God and the ever-active Spirit of Evil.

Certain particular reasons, however, hold good in the case of the Jesuits, of which two or three may be alleged.

Opposition at the hands of the world, from the unthinking as well as from the openly irreligious, may be simply ascribed to the fact that the Jesuit's lot in life is closely assimilated to the lot of the active life of Christ on earth, to that phase of His life during which He encountered actual opposition, and which culminated in His Passion and Death. This was the lot of the Apostles, who in like manner shared His active, rather than His hidden and, if we may say so, unaggressive life. Just as opposition was predicted by its Founder for the Church in general, so for the Apostles a particular vehemence of onslaught was predicted. "They will put you out of the synagogues: yea, the hour cometh, that whosoever killeth you, will think that he doth a service to God."

To experience such opposition is not pleasanter for a Jesuit than for anybody else. On the contrary, it becomes harder to endure when long years in the service of his fellow-man have taught one the sublime value of human friendship, the inestimable privilege of cooperation and harmony with all men. Especially grievous is calumny, misinterpretation and sullen dislike to one who sees the harm that men do to *themselves* by such a state of mind, when one sees good works ruined by some subjective antipathy, that have cost years of intelligent labor, and have brought consolation to the poor, enlightenment to the ignorant, and have laid the foundations of social justice and lasting temporal as well as spiritual happiness for thousands. The ruined Reductions of Paraguay, the shattered university halls of Mexico, and the blood-stained soil of Nanking bear witness to man's inhumanity to himself.

Nevertheless, great as is the sorrow that such persecution causes a thinking man, the thoughts of the Religious man are calmed and steadied even in the most sudden onslaught by the thought that what is momentarily experienced was prophesied by the Master Himself two thousand years ago. Though in vastly lesser degree, it is the logical sharing in His own condition on earth, which is the essence of the great Adventure, and, as He Himself observed, "the servant shall not be greater than the Master."

Tactlessness, imprudence or vanity on the part of individual Jesuits at various epochs may be alleged. Yet where such exist—and they are found in every group of men—they have been clearly seen to be working against the spirit of the Order, not in line with it.

II

Why, however, should the Society experience opposition frequently not only from the malevolent, but from the good and well-intentioned in the Church—for the fact is undeniable?

The obvious answer lies in the aggressive character of the Jesuit apostolate, as seeking and maintaining the "outposts," and therefore rousing good men often from too much sense of security, disturbing them by unwelcome warnings, and urging others to action who would prefer to be left at rest.

Beside this evident reason, however, there is another less obvious which, I think, has much to do with the uncomfortable feelings entertained by some perfectly well-intentioned Catholics towards the Jesuit Order. The Society as such is devoted to the Universal Church, rather than to any particular locality. In all questions where the interests of the Church and humanity at large come in conflict with those of a particular limited group of men, the Society places the weight of its activity and influence where the larger and broader interest may be served, and thereby *in the end* secure the greater welfare of the locality as well. For not only *a priori* reasoning, but actual experience shows that when the larger interest is sacrificed for the good of a fraction, the smaller part invariably atrophies and withers up in the end.

The long conflict which the Society of Jesus endured in France, for the century previous to its Suppression in 1760, was chiefly a disagreement between a mistaken idea of national religious interests supposedly represented by

Gallicanism, and the vital and fruitful view of the Universal Church as truly one, to which the Jesuit Order was committed in policy as well as in theory. The ecclesiastical resistance against the wholeness and the oneness of the Church triumphed, at least externally, over the Society of Jesus, but the result for France was the French Revolution and the official apostasy of the nation. The return to practical and vital religion, the marvelous religious renaissance of France in recent years, has been and is still along the path long since pointed out by those, who even before the Vatican Council, saw the true interest of France to lie in close union with the life-giving source of vital religious unity, the Holy See, as the center of the Universal Church.

How self-defeating is the spirit of particularism may be seen today from the condition of the Near East, where the different national and autonomous Churches among our separated Orthodox brethren lie prostrate under the weight of those secular conditions, to which they surrendered not only their independence, but their religious life as well, in departing from the vital unity of the Church.

Moreover, whatever cause may be assigned for the opposition experienced by Jesuits at various periods of their history, there is also the fact that being united, as a Religious family, in a particularly close bond of union, the entire body suffers to some extent from the distress felt by any one part. Where the group in a Religious family is largely local, as in a restricted territory, or still more in a single monastery, the periphery of exposure to contradiction is correspondingly restricted. The opportunity also for giving real or fancied offence is just so much the smaller. But where the family *as a family*, one and closely united, is nevertheless spread out over the entire world, in every conceivable human circumstance and in contact with every possible variety of human interests and passions, the occasions from which a contradiction may arise are innumerable.

However, though perfectly good *men* have opposed the Society, opposition is rarely, if ever felt, from actual *forces for good*, as such. On the contrary, the Jesuit experiences the power of cooperation with all good men, and none are more ready and apt to cooperate with all good movements, within as well as without the Church.

This applies not merely to works of a distinctly religious character, such as the work of the Foreign and Home Missions, the various works for Catholic education, etc. It applies also to undertakings where Catholics and non-Catholics take part for the common welfare. To take a few instances in our own country: the marvelous work for youth conducted by the City of New York in its camps on the Hudson River, has had as one of its chief promoters a Jesuit. In the field of hospital and other institutional endeavors American Jesuits similar to all American Catholic clergymen cooperate constantly with other denominations and with State and municipal authorities for the welfare of the sick, the insane, and the dependent.

III

This brings one finally to the interesting question, is the Jesuit Order a static or a progressive institution? Since this particular yardstick is whipped out at a moment's notice to settle the final scores of everything from a Pyramid to a postage-stamp, it is well to see just what progress can be measured for that body of men who in the minds of many spell conservatism or even retrogression.

Before further consideration it is well to remember that the opposition experienced during his lifetime by the Founder of the Society from good and even saintly men was due precisely to the fact that he was an innovator. If the Society occasionally wears a conservative aspect today, it wore a far from conservative aspect in its origin. The proposal to do away with the Religious habit and wear no prescribed dress, and to substitute the private recitation of the Breviary for the public chant or recitation of the Office in choir, were considered not only as revolutionary, but as radically destructive of the very essence of the Religious life. This, moreover, was in a time and country where the Religious life and observance were as familiar to the man in the street as the policeman's uniform is today.

But even at the present day, when the echoes of such canonical controversies have long since passed away, the Jesuit Order can be termed conservative only in the positive sense, of having an inheritance of human and Divine values to preserve, but in no wise in the negative meaning of opposing or retarding true progress.

If we mean by progress a perpetual process of self-transformation, in which the whole as well as the parts are continually remodelled, then the Society of Jesus, like any other Order, is not progressive. In that sense the human organism is not progressive, for it remains ever the same, though with new assimilation of material and numberless minor changes. If, however, we mean that the principles which guided the Society at its beginning take on a continually wider application with the progress of time, then the Society is not only progressive, but is anticipatory of the future.

Each new age brings new applications for the principles underlying the Jesuit apostolate. With these new applications comes a new understanding as to the meaning of these principles. This newer and deeper understanding leads in turn to new applications of old truths, corresponding to the needs of the times. Hence, though the Religious family remains true to its original type, though its traditions remain intact, the fuller grasp of what these traditions really mean leads to a genuine progress, as is the case of the Church in general, which is continually progressing to a more and more perfect realization, in the sphere of history, of the plan of her Divine Founder.

To choose one out of many obvious examples, we may consider the twentieth-century undertaking of workingmen's Retreats, in which, besides the assistance given to the retreatants in the purely spiritual order, some of the principles of Catholic social doctrine are inculcated. The existence of industrial workers as a distinct group in society is a phase of modern life. Their social problems are correspondingly new. New also is the timely interpretation of old doctrines and principles given, let us say, by Pope Leo XIII in his famous Encyclical on the "Condition of the Workingman." In the application to this group of that typical form of the apostolate known as the Closed Retreat, the very doctrines of the Exercises are seen in a wider bearing, in their relation to the problems of the pres-

ent day, and in their relation also to the more recent pro-
nouncements of the Church.

Hence not only new applications are found of those
original doctrines, as personally taught and personally realized by the first Fathers of the Jesuit Order, but new activities in behalf of the workingman spring up as a result.
Members of the Order are set aside to study these modern
problems. Periodicals, scientific or popular, originate for
their discussion or publicity. Practical social works to
meet special needs originate, such as workingmen's clubs,
associations for youth, workingmen's study-circles, libra-
ries, etc. The field of trades unionism, of anti-communist
propaganda, of parish missions for workingmen's districts,
of Catholic action in all its manifold phases, offers an almost indefinite development of the original simple type of
the apostolate. Yet it is a development, and application,
not an alteration or a diminishing of the original type.

Together with this development comes an assimilation
of all elements of the good in the way of knowledge and
art that assist in the service of one's fellow-man. There is
no truly cultural element of value which has not its place
in the work of furthering the spiritual welfare of one's
neighbor. This assimilation of the truly good, of those
things which in themselves are good, is the opposite of a
spirit of expediency which would make use of doubtful

and questionable elements, in the hope that they might somehow be sanctified by the object for which they are used. Such a spirit of expediency is not only not known to the Society, but is the very opposite of its true spirit.

In the physical world whatever has life is characterized by growth, so that in no respect to grow is to cease to live. It grows by taking into its own substance external materials; and this absorption or assimilation is completed when the materials appropriated come to belong to it or enter into its unity . . . Thus, a power of development is a power of life, not only in its essay, but especially in its success; for a mere formula either does not expand or is shattered in expanding. A living idea becomes many, yet remains one. (Newman, *Development of Christian Doctrine*, p. 185.)

Such assimilation of the good of every epoch is the spirit of Christianity itself. Else there would be no meaning in the scholarship of St. Jerome or the architecture of St. Sophia.

Yet, as history shows, there is always a danger that in the assimilation of the good there may be a mistaken appropriation of the bad. The most imposing elements in a generation may be more chaff than wheat. In the Constitutions of the Society preachers and writers were warned against adopting the artificial compliments of the Court, or the stilted phraseology current in the sermons of the sixteenth century. Similar dangers exist today, on account of the reign of half-truths in modern thought. Sublimated forms of materialism and sensuality are spread over the world with great ease. Under the guise of science unscientific panaceas for delicate and complex social problems are peddled about. Living in the public eye, the educator, the preacher, the writer, are called to account if they fail to respect some formula or undigested theory which has caught the popular fancy for the moment. Men are called conservative, by the so-called radicals, for doubting the wisdom of some political or social theory which was practised by Hammurabi or Rameses the Great, and resulted in confusion and failure in the past. Or they are called radical and revolutionary by interested seekers for personal gain, because they wish to safeguard the rights of the poor man and the toiler by appealing to the age-old landmarks of Christian justice.

The Jesuit, as we have seen, meets the ideas of men on the outposts, in the fields of the greatest resistance, not as filtered down through the discriminating wisdom of others who have previously encountered them and sifted out the good from the bad, as the colors of the garish sunlight are sifted down through the mellowing medium of the Cathedral window. His office is to initiate the discrimination, not to profit by it; and for this task great personal faithfulness to inner prayer and the guiding spirit of his Constitutions is necessary. In the last analysis, the wisdom and courage needed for this task are the fruit of humility.

How far individual Jesuits have shown lack of discrimination in the past, thereby in some manner compromising the good name of their Religious family, is a matter for historical judgment, into which this sketch does not enter. Where such mistakes have occurred, as they are bound to occur as long as men are mortal, they are due not to the spirit of the Church nor the spirit of the Society, but to its neglect—in some cases lack of vigilance of Superiors, or lack of proper admission or training of individuals. But like all such phenomena they excite interest and attention for the very reason that they *are* exceptions, and are clearly seen as foreign not only to the spirit of the Religious family, but to the vast body of its actual traditions and observance.

Although the Society of Jesus exposes its members to special perils of contagion, if one may use that ancient metaphor, from the spirit of half-truth and compromise latent in the world in which the Apostleship must be wrought out, there are also special helps given to overcome this peril, and form a spirit of resistance to evil and the danger of subtle decay. For together with familiarity with the danger is also a spirit of awareness to it, and a passion of love for the primitive ideals by which its first members were banded together. The personal practice of the Spiritual Exercises is especially a perpetual means of regeneration. By means of them every Jesuit is reminded every year as long as he lives of the primitive ideals of the Order. Some fifteen years after the restoration of the Society, the first work of Father Roothaan, then Superior General of the Order, was to ensure its spiritual restoration—without which its merely legal existence would have been fruitless—by means of the original text of the group of spiritual memoranda known as the Book of the Spiritual Exercises, and the earnest interpretation of them to every member of the Jesuit family as the principal means of spiritual renewal.

Moreover, the Religious bodies of the Catholic Church, since they are grounded on the Faith, do not look upon themselves without respect to the Faith. They do not count on purely human means either of growth or of subsistence. If they did, none would endure beyond a single generation. They are each part of the vital constitution of the Church as a whole: not merely within the Church, but part of her integral framework. Hence they share as parts something of the life-giving promise given to the Church as a whole: not, it is true, her infallibility, or her existence to the end of time, yet they look for a measure of Divine guidance, for the inner enlightenment and protection of the Holy Spirit, and the efficacy of means of sanctification which are not wholly of human origin.

Were any one of them to decay, to suffer degradation from its primitive ideal, no other part of the Church can conceivably profit by it in any way whatsoever, any more than the body can profit by the decay or withering of any one of its members. Each part thrives by the life-giving sap which flows through the entire body, and, in turn, the power, the vitality and efficacy of every part of the Church as a whole is indefinitely increased by the flourishing state of each humblest member of its entire organism.

EPILOGUE

In the year 1934, the three hundredth anniversary will be celebrated of the landing and first Mass of the Maryland Pilgrims on March 25, 1634, on St. Clement's Island. The new establishment at St. Mary's City, of which Father White and Father Altham were the first spiritual guides, was the first to profess religious liberty in the New World. From there, by a process of orderly expansion, came not only the growth of the Society of Jesus in the American Colonies, but, through the Jesuit canonical establishment in Southern Maryland, and the person of John Carroll, the first Archbishop of Baltimore, came also the development of the American Hierarchy, and the spread of the Catholic Church throughout a great part of the United States.

Since the Restoration of the Society of Jesus at the beginning of the nineteenth century it has spread to the whole United States. There are at present 3,418 members working in thirty-six dioceses and archdioceses of this country. Twenty-two colleges and universities, thirty-six high-schools, and eighty-five residences are in charge of the Society.